To: Pearl

From: Olie

1/1/97

# The Feminine Journey

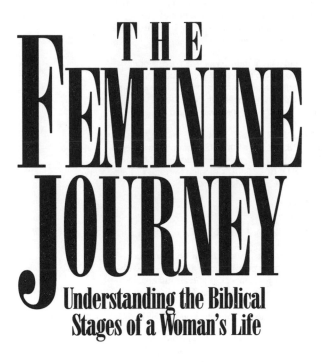

# THE FEMININE JOURNEY

## Understanding the Biblical
## Stages of a Woman's Life

# Cynthia & Robert Hicks

NAVPRESS
BRINGING TRUTH TO LIFE
NavPress Publishing Group
P.O. Box 35001, Colorado Springs, Colorado 80935

The Navigators is an international Christian organization. Jesus Christ gave His followers the Great Commission to go and make disciples (Matthew 28:19). The aim of The Navigators is to help fulfill that commission by multiplying laborers for Christ in every nation.

NavPress is the publishing ministry of The Navigators. NavPress publications are tools to help Christians grow. Although publications alone cannot make disciples or change lives, they can help believers learn biblical discipleship, and apply what they learn to their lives and ministries.

Library of Congress Catalog Card Number:
        94-4480
ISBN 08910-97708

Cover illustration: Shelley A. Webb

Some of the anecdotal illustrations in this book are true to life and are included with the permission of the persons involved. All other illustrations are composites of real situations, and any resemblance to people living or dead is coincidental.

Unless otherwise identified, all Scripture quotations in this publication are taken from the *New American Standard Bible* (NASB), © The Lockman Foundation 1960, 1962, 1963, 1968, 1971, 1972, 1973, 1975, 1977. Other versions used include: the *HOLY BIBLE: NEW INTERNATIONAL VERSION* ® (NIV®), Copyright © 1973, 1978, 1984 by International Society, used by permission of Zondervan Publishing House, all rights reserved; and the *King James Version* (KJV).

Printed in the United States of America

Hicks, Cynthia.
        The feminine journey : understanding the biblical
stages of a woman's life / by Cynthia and Robert Hicks.
        p. cm.
        Includes bibliographical references.
        ISBN 0-89109-770-8
        1. Women—Religious life. 2. Woman (Christian theol-
ogy) I. Hicks, Robert (Robert H.) II. Title.
BV4527.H49   1994
248.8'43—dc20                                      94-4480
                                                    CIP

FOR A FREE CATALOG OF
NAVPRESS BOOKS & BIBLE STUDIES,
CALL 1-800-366-7788 (USA)
or 1-416-499-4615 (CANADA)

# CONTENTS

*Dedicated to the women*
*who have made my feminine journey*
*a trip worth taking:*

*To my mother, Ann Rosenburg, for being the bearer*
*of both my physical and spiritual birth.*
*I rise up and call you blessed.*

*To my daughter Charis,*
*my first born and soul mate.*

*To my daughter Ashley,*
*my calm and sunshine amid the storm.*

*To my sisters—*
*Cathy, I cannot image life without my twin.*
*We journey side by side.*
*Lori, a chip off the old block.*
*Mer lives through you.*

# ACKNOWLEDGMENTS

Having dedicated this book to the women in my life, I want to remember these wonderful men.

I thank my husband, Bob, whose assistance, encouragement, and patience made this manuscript a reality. You know my struggles as no one else does. I love you for what we've had and for what is yet to come.

To my son, Graham, may you grow to appreciate the feminine side of life.

I want to acknowledge the men in our extended family. Thanks to my brother, Charlie, for your listening ear and words of advice.

To my brothers-in-law, Billy and Bob, thanks just for being who you are.

Thanks goes to my son-in-law Jason. Your sweet spirit and love for Charis gives me more joy than you know.

Thanks goes to Steve Griffith. You were there the night *The Feminine Journey* was born.

Thanks also to Steve Webb, our senior editor, who believed enough in us to have a go with this book. It's a privilege to be a part of your team.

Lastly, I acknowledge those fellow travelers, whose stories of struggle, courage, and survival breathed life into this manuscript. Although the names have been changed, you will see yourself in these pages.

# AUTHORS

❦

Born Cynthia Ann Bliss, "Cinny" spent her formative years in Winter Park, Florida. In high school she was active in sports and school government. Following graduation, she attended college in South Carolina, then went on to the University of Florida, where she majored in sociology. After college, she toured with a nationally known singing group. She also developed and led women's ministries at the University of Pennsylvania and the University of Hawaii. She has done continuing education at the University of Hawaii and Dallas Theological Seminary.

Cinny has appeared on network television, including "Charlie's Angels," "Dallas," and "The Sally Jesse Rafael Show." She has also done local television commercials. She has worked in the apparel industry, done network marketing, and currently manages an interior decorating business.

Cinny is a widely requested speaker for motivational seminars, and with her husband has conducted conferences throughout the United States and abroad. She coauthored articles on friendship and marriage, which are published in the book *Husbands and Wives*.

Dr. Robert Hicks is professor of Pastoral Theology at the Seminary of the East in Philadelphia. He cofounded Life Counseling Services and served as a chaplain with the Air National Guard. In 1985, Bob was honored with the American Legion nomination for "Chaplain of the Year," an award presented by President Reagan for Bob's work with the families and survivors of the Delta 191 crash at Dallas-Ft. Worth Airport.

He has authored *Uneasy Manhood* (Nelson, 1991), *Returning Home* (Revell, 1991), and *Failure to Scream* (Nelson, 1993). He holds degrees in psychology, theology, and family studies and has pursued post-doctoral work in religious studies at Villanova University.

Bob and Cinny reside in a Philadelphia suburb and have three children—two daughters and one son.

# FOREWORD

*Relevant, thoughtful, and enlightening.*

That will be your response to this book. Together Bob and Cinny have done a masterful job of exploring the impact of our culture upon a woman's search for identity. They have presented us with a clear, sensible, refreshing description of six aspects of growth and development that we women experience in our journey toward maturity.

Over the last twenty years there has been much confusion among women as we seek to understand ourselves and our role in society.

While many Christian women tend to "write off" much of the women's movement, the revolutionary changes going on among women have certainly impacted all women in our culture regardless of their spiritual, social, or political outlook.

Instead of "throwing out" the message of the feminist movement, Bob and Cinny "draw on it" to help us better understand who we are as women in Christ.

One of the positive developments among sociologists and psychologists has been a slightly different way of looking at the process of maturity and fulfillment in life. Through a "developmental" view of life, we come to understand that we don't just move from childhood to adulthood to old age but that we tend to move through aspects or passages in life.

The Hicks have helped those of us who hold to scriptural authority to bring this broader understanding of adulthood to our own lives, while presenting it to us from a biblical perspective.

The book looks at six aspects of womanhood: the creational woman, the young woman, the nurturer, the relational woman, the wounded woman, and the woman of strength. By understanding these aspects derived from six Hebrew words used for "woman" in the Bible, we are reminded that these different aspects of a woman's life are not new but have been here since the time of the book of Genesis.

*The Feminine Journey* is not a prescriptive book—telling us what to do—but an analytical book—helping us to understand ourselves.

Throughout the book examples of contemporary and biblical women are used. For instance, I found a new kinship with Eve as I identified with her tendency toward dissatisfaction.

Cinny is refreshingly honest about her own self doubts. She tells of her personal anger and pain caused by fellow church members and her frustrations with her own perceived role as a Christian wife.

Her explanations of the differences between men and women will make you laugh. Her description of the wounded woman contains an unusual sensitivity to the pain of those who have been widowed or suffered from abuse or divorce.

While reading *The Feminine Journey,* you will find yourself thinking, *That's me. She's saying what I've felt but haven't been able to articulate.*

This is a book for any woman, whatever her circumstance—whether single, married, or in the later years of life. It will be of special encouragement to those involved in Christian ministry.

The fact that this book has been written for women by a husband and wife team is extremely significant. Bob brings a masculine balance to a women's view of femininity, which is so helpful. Just as Bob's book *The Masculine Journey* gives insight to women and to men, this book, while written primarily to women, will enable men to better understand women.

My husband, John, and I have known Bob and Cinny for over twenty-five years. Their life together has demonstrated for us and for countless others, the strength that comes from walking in obedience to Christ regardless of the circumstances. When so many are falling away, they have chosen to be faithful to the calling of God on their lives.

Their careful, scholarly, yet practical analysis given in this book has a ring of truth for me.

After reading this book, you will walk away thankful for the incredibly complicated way that God has made you and with the assurance that your own experience in life is not so different from that of countless other women.

—SUSAN A. YATES

# CHAPTER ONE

# A WOMAN'S UNEASY JOURNEY

❧

*In the middle of the journey of our life, I came to myself
within a dark wood where the straight way was lost.*
DANTE

*The longest journey is the journey inwards.*
DAG HAMMERSKJOLD

Our family had been invited by an organization to go to Australia for the summer and speak on family topics. Bob, who teaches at a theological seminary, decided to take several of his students with us so they could gain valuable experience as they worked with students at the University of Sydney. The trip would fulfill certain degree requirements for their internship while also providing life-stretching cross-cultural experiences.

Australia is not a place I had ever envisioned visiting. However, the children were excited about taking such a long trip. Also, our students were such an interesting mix of personalities that I looked forward to spending time with them and having the adventure of a lifetime. Little did I know what I was in for.

Over the years before this trip, Bob and I did a great deal of speaking and teaching. I always enjoyed sharing the platform with him, and usually felt confident and excited about what I had to say. Shyness and lack of something to say have never been problems for me. As Joan Rivers says, "I enter talking." In addition, you can count on my thoughts to be delivered with great enthusiasm and passion!

This unexpected journey for our family threw me into a tailspin in terms of thinking about what clothing items each person needed to take. Packing for a family of five for a two-month trip halfway around the world from Dallas, Texas, consumed my thoughts. Though it was to be summer in Dallas, it would be winter in Australia. Bob's suggestion to all of us was that no one take more luggage than he or she was able to manage personally. Those who travel overseas understand the wisdom of this thinking. Contrary to what Americans think, there is not always a porter or other person available to handle the overload of luggage. Of course this has never worried me because I always have Bob!

Due to going to a foreign country, special accessories were necessary for electrical items like hair dryers and curling irons. Our children were still young. Charis was thirteen, Ashley was eleven, and Graham was seven. So there were also toys, books, and other fun items to consider. Needless to say, we ended up taking half of what I planned, and it was still too much! However, for women—at least this woman—it is very important that one be prepared for anything. Women understand this in a way that men never will.

Upon arriving in Australia, we went through a few days of briefing on the country, learning about the uniqueness of the Australian people, their history, and current issues. The seminary students were chomping at the bit to get started. Half of them were to spend a month in Sydney and half were to go to a small mining town in Broken Hill, part of the famous (or infamous) Australian outback. Our family spent a month in Sydney and then went to Broken Hill.

Sydney is a very cosmopolitan city, quite European in fashion. People take trains almost everywhere due to the high cost of gasoline and cars. If they drive, it's on the "wrong" side of the street. I found grocery stores to be expensive and rather uninteresting compared to our mega stores in Dallas. I chose to visit mostly the specialty stores: the beef shop, the bakery, and the fruit and vegetable stands. Many people buy their groceries for the evening meal on their way home, at the little shops surrounding the various train stations.

## STRANGE SURROUNDINGS AND STRANGE FEELINGS

Amid the fun and excitement of the trip I began to experience new feelings of fear, anxiety, intimidation, and reluctance each time Bob and I were to speak. Granted, there were cultural differences that could cause some expected reactions, but my feelings were well beyond that.

One night before I was to speak to a group of women, I suddenly was filled with panic, inadequacy, and fear. I just could not do it. I was in tears, and Bob tried to encourage me. My subject matter was familiar, having given this talk many times before. Here I was, the seminary professor's wife, the main speaker, and I was too afraid to speak.

Two of the students with us were very competent women, working on their master's degrees. I had also met several Australian women who were excellent communicators. I was simply immobilized by feelings of inadequacy and couldn't understand why. Other than a radio interview Bob and I did together at the end of the trip, I did not attempt to do any more speaking.

The trip proved to be a memorable one for our family in many positive ways. It was one of those shared experiences that we will talk about for the rest of our lives. However, for me the trip was far more than a journey to a foreign country. I also began a journey of self-doubt, insecurity, mid-life crisis, and emotional and spiritual turmoil that is just now beginning to simmer down.

## END OF THE TRIP BUT NOT THE JOURNEY

It has been almost nine years since the trip to Australia. Those years have been a difficult period of growth for me. As I reflect on that time, Australia was just the place where I happened to be when I became aware of some latent issues that had been stirring in me for years.

I was almost twenty when I was confronted with the spiritual side of life and entered into a relationship with Christ. I'd had little church experience up to that point. When I married Bob, who chose the ministry as his vocation, I was unprepared and unrealistic in my expectations and understanding of ministry as well as life.

For many years I tried very hard to be the kind of person I thought others expected of a pastor's wife. During the years of Bob's graduate school, several moves and disappointments apparently took their toll on me. What happened next was just the straw that broke this camel's back. Today, I am grateful for the brokenness, the painful confrontations, and the insights that have been gained.

As a young adult I had considered myself to be happy, cooperative, and energetic. I viewed life with optimism and a belief that I was strong enough to accomplish whatever needed to be done. I then realized that the point had come in my life to put away the childish notions and journey on as an adult.

From Dallas we moved to the Philadelphia area. The move to Pennsylvania promised to be positive and exciting for the entire family. A large church had pursued Bob quite persistently, hoping to have him join their church staff. It was not easy for Bob to leave the seminary position he loved, but this just seemed like the Lord's leading. The church was located in an affluent suburban area outside of Philadelphia, where the public school system was heralded as one of the top in the country. We saw an opportunity to expose our children to a little culture in an historic location as well as to experience the beautiful surroundings and four distinct seasons.

We had been in the church only for a couple of months when we suddenly became aware of major staff problems. After two years of turmoil the senior pastor resigned, other staff left, and the church experienced an explosive split. During this crisis, Bob was asked to be the interim preaching pastor. For the next year and a half, he preached almost every Sunday.

My emotions had been bumped around significantly during the previous two years due to the disruption of the church staff. I had been involved for years in various ministries teaching the Bible. However, now it seemed as if my experience was being brought into question. Apparently I was not qualified to teach because I had not been through a specific program in the church. There were misunderstandings, I felt hurt and unappreciated, and consequently withdrew. It was discouraging for me to have prepared for and participated in ministry for many years and then be viewed as one unprepared to serve.

I felt anger and resentment, and blamed my feelings on a lack of acceptance, plus the difficulties that Bob experienced. There were also conflicts with the leadership that were hard for me to swallow. Our children fell under the typical "preacher's kids" scrutiny. Finally, I decided these petty people who felt it their duty to be the watchdogs of the church would do better to attend to their own homes and be less critical of those God had called to serve.

As a result, Bob left the church and took a teaching position at a local seminary. I was emotionally distraught, feeling victimized, powerless, and ready to pull out of ministry altogether. I had poured twenty years into ministry with Bob and couldn't believe that God would let our family go through so much turmoil. I felt we had made a big mistake in moving to the Northeast. I was angry within myself and so hurt I could not attend the church without constantly crying and feeling confused. I simply fell apart both emotionally and spiritually. I didn't know who I was anymore, or what God wanted me to do. I did not feel capable of doing much of anything. Feelings of inadequacy, shame, guilt, and fear loomed within. I had to make a change and I did.

For four years I left the world of ministry and got involved in business. I seldom attended church or sought any Christian fellowship. I isolated myself from anything that was not associated with my business. I pulled away from my children and from my husband. I decided I was going to "find myself."

Isn't this what the feminist movement has been telling women of today to do? I hoped I would find my value and self-worth in working, accomplishing goals, and making money. Little did I realize that through this process I would emotionally seal myself off from my family and my God.

Those four years are now a blur to me. In her book *The Revolution from Within,* Gloria Steinem reveals her discovery that throughout her years of dedicated involvement in the women's movement she suffered from low self-esteem. Her work in the political arena in seeking to give women a new vision for themselves was just her way of coping with her past and compensating for the pain. In describing her life during this time, she writes that she was living "like a soldier who is wounded but won't lie down for fear of dying. I just kept marching."[1]

Now, I'm not a big fan of Gloria Steinem, but I was amazed by her open disclosure. Here was a woman who had been in the battle for women's rights and seemed so self-confident, but was now coming up short within herself. Ms. Steinem had it all: education, success, career, achievements, honors, and acclaim. This did not heal the sense of woundedness and low self-esteem. Could it be that the quest for a woman's self-esteem was not to be found in merely gaining equality with men? Ms. Steinem's confession raised for me the interesting question of whether a woman's self-esteem is necessarily found in her actions or in her fundamental being.

As I look back on everything now, I think I was driven to keep busy throughout my life. Perhaps I am one of those personalities who escape into the lives of others rather than dealing with my own life issues. However, I do believe God wants us to be personally responsible on this journey for our own life in order to be healthy in our motivations and involvements with others. Some of the insights revealed to me during those years made me see that healthy changes needed to be made.

However, the "finding of myself" took a toll on my family. I had changed the family system; I was different. Gail Sheehy wrote a classic work on women's issues entitled *Passages: Predictable Crises of Adult Life.* In it she writes, "With each passage (or transition from one stage to another in life) some magic must be given up, some cherished illusion of safety and comfortably familiar sense of self must be cast off to allow for the greater expansion of our own distinctiveness."[2] She goes on to say, "We must be willing to change chairs if we want to grow. There is no right chair. What is right at one stage may be restricting at another or too soft."[3]

My pendulum had swung from being a wife and a mother who was so involved in the lives of her husband and children that she had no identity of her own, to being a working woman who saw herself only as an individual who happened to have three children and a husband. In the last two years I have been reexamining my responsibilities as a woman, wife, mother, and Christian. I'm reminding myself that life is a journey and I've just been moving from chair to chair.

I've come to see that my feelings of anger directed at the Christian community were due to my perception of the traditional Christian role for women, which had let me down. Bob and I had committed our adult lives to being as prepared and open as possible to serving the Lord. And yet, at every turn of the road we experienced pitfalls in the form of critical people, judgmental attitudes, and insensitivity. I found I did not have a strong enough grasp of who I was in Christ, or my own beliefs about what God wanted from me, to survive and function well. In addition, I held the erroneous belief that life would be a smooth journey and I would eventually be rewarded for all my personal sacrifices. I felt I had paid my price and now it was God's turn to give us what I thought we deserved.

I loved Philip Yancy's book *Disappointment with God* because the title expressed my sentiments perfectly.[4] I was disappointed with God. I thought we had left a good job to walk into a hornet's nest. Bob had been used, abused, then tossed aside. Our children had been hurt and lost interest in the church at a critical developmental period in their lives. I had been made to feel inferior, worthless, and powerless.

To make matters worse during this time of struggle, I felt I couldn't really share how I was feeling with anyone in the church family. I have always felt the need to keep certain problems hidden. We weren't supposed to have marriage problems or rebellious children. I was afraid to be honest with others about our problems for fear of how it would reflect on my husband. (If a man can't take care of his own house, how can he take care of the house of God?— 1 Timothy 3:4-5.) I honestly felt that to share family difficulties would put Bob's job on the line. I realize now that none of our difficulties was anything out of the ordinary for the average marriage or parents raising teenagers. I just wouldn't allow us to be human. I was plagued by a sense of failure, fearing that others would not accept my human frailties. This was a tough, impossible burden for me and unfair of me to place it on my family.

Now I realize this whole experience was just a stage on my journey, but one that took time to figure out. My pain had driven me into a dark, cold cave. I was dissatisfied, isolated, and depressed. I couldn't believe the normally positive, upbeat Cinny was in a state of depression. I felt as though my journey was over, that I was just walking through a fog, staying busy and not feeling anything.

During what was such a difficult time for me, Bob had continued to be productive and had entered the world of publishing. He has now written four books, two of which deal with men's issues. These projects were very therapeutic for him during his own journey through those difficult times.

That's one reason we decided that it was time for me to explore on paper the journey of a woman's life. Although I continue to battle with the impossible load of perfectionism, I think I can now better navigate this journey. Perhaps my journey will also be of help to my fellow sisters. My encouragement to others is expressed in Nancy Groom's book *From Bondage to Bonding*, where she writes, "The world needs to see honest strugglers, not pious pretenders."[5]

I am at the midway point on my life journey. I think I have asked the questions most women ask, have experienced the ups and the downs of the journey, and feel I've made a few discoveries along the way that can be helpful to others. My main desire is to be a real person, to be vulnerable and honest about the struggles I have experienced while also giving tribute to the grace and sufficiency of God, who has brought me this far.

It's a wonderful thing as one gets older that there is neither the energy nor the inclination to play games. You gain perspective and realize that everyone is running on the same merry-go-round. We're all in this journey of life together, and we'll make it through with less pain and more joy if we do it together.

C. Day Lewis wrote, "We do not write in order to be understood, but we write in order to understand."[6] Through an exploration of the biblical terms that give us insights into God's conception of a woman's journey, I hope that another light might be turned on to illuminate my reader's path.

Life is a journey, "a traveling from one place to another," according to one dictionary. The Old Testament is laced through with the wanderings and journeys of God's people. The picture is one of pilgrimage, traveling from place to place toward a shrine or holy place. Every journey has a beginning, a middle, and an end. Some of us forget the starting place as we focus on the final destination. Unfortunately, we lose sight of the value of the process in the journey.

"Most of life is lived along the way," according to M. Craig Barnes in his insightful and profound book, *Yearning*. Barnes goes on to say, "What distinguishes Christians from the world is not that we have figured out how to live more successfully, more fully, or even more securely than the non-Christian. . . . The promise God fulfills now is that in our discipleship we will find new meaning and vision for our lives."[7] We know that we will see God at the end of this journey, but we forget we don't have to wait until the end to experience God. It is through the process, day by day, that God is glorified and reveals Himself to us.

Not only are we on a journey, but as believers in Jesus Christ, we part company with others in that this earthly world is not our final resting place. There is a higher calling. The Bible declares us to be "strangers and exiles on the earth" (Hebrews 11:13). It's not easy being an exile in a foreign land. The voices from a completely secularized and psychologized world would put women on a journey toward self-awareness and self-happiness. This makes the chief end for women a finding of fulfillment, good feelings, and a self that needs to be actualized (whatever that means). My conversations with women reveal that education, work outside the home, and making money have failed us and left us as dissatisfied as men (who also have sought such things).

Some believe the traditional "Christian" perspective has also deceived women with the teaching that our *only* significance should lie in our connection with our husband and children, with little or no value placed on the development of personal identity. As a result, a conflict has emerged between two ideologies that, when taken to extremes, hopelessly fail women.

I believe most women today are journeying somewhere between

the feminist camp and the strict Christian "woman at home" camp. Certainly, a woman's concern and her responsibilities toward her family are important. This is often the longest stop on the feminine journey unless altered, complicated, or completed before a woman is ready to move on. Divorce, the loss of children, illness, loss of the husband's job, his death, and other unexpected events can thrust a woman's life into a different season immediately.

And we must consider the journeys of single (never-married) women whose identities and callings are vitally important to God, and who make up a large and growing part of today's culture. I believe all women need a greater sense of who they are individually apart from their primary relationships. I believe we need to see that we possess an important identity as people designed by our Creator. Single women, incidentally, may be in the best position to realize this and benefit from it.

## THE DEVELOPMENTAL JOURNEY

In recent years both the educational and psychological communities have taken a second look at this thing called "adulthood." When I was in school, we were taught that life was essentially divided into three developmental periods: child, adolescent, and adult. Somewhere between the ages of nineteen and twenty-five (a guess) a woman became an adult for the rest of her life.

Today, this static view of adult life has changed. Adulthood is now recognized as having its own shape, seasons, and stages.[8] Just as the arrival of fall gives us an anticipation of what lies ahead in winter (leaves falling, raking, cooler temperatures, dressing appropriately), so adult life has its own developmental phases. One researcher says all of life is "the product of interaction between growing human organisms and its environment."[9] Since our interactions and environment are constantly changing, we as adults must also see life as developmental change.

Gail Sheehy, author of *Passages,* views this developmental journey in more internal terms. She writes, "A developmental stage, however, is not defined in terms of marker events; it is defined by changes that begin within. The underlying impulse toward change will be there regardless of whether or not it is manifested in or accentuated by a marker event."[10]

For me, the changes began within, making me realize that my life was taking on a different shape and I was entering a different season. As Bob says in his book *The Masculine Journey,* understanding life as a journey suggests that at every new place encountered there is a time of temporary confusion, a time to separate from the past and undergo some kind of initiation into the next stage. In every season some developmental tasks will probably be required. Some adjustment time is the norm, in order to keep us moving on the journey without getting stuck or lost in the developmental mud.[11] As in all developmental literature, there must be some ultimate goal toward which all growth is directed. I will attempt to clarify what I believe to be the biblical goal as well as the developmental goal for women.

Should our goal as women be to be as beautiful as possible, or to get married, or to have children, or to run a business, or to retire in comfort? These may be worthy short-term goals, but should any of these be the dominant ambition for our lives? Hopefully, in seeing these ambitions as but seasons of a woman's life we can be better prepared for the time when they disappoint us or are completely taken away.

Women today are inundated with various maps to guide us on our journey. Which map should we chose? What luggage do we need to take with us? After all, our final destination does determine what we need to bring along. Finally, what equipment has the Master Designer given His female creation to best prepare us and use us on this journey? We are different from our male counterparts. Our needs, abilities, and talents are unique to us alone.

In this book, *The Feminine Journey,* I will explore and illumine six aspects of what it means to be a woman journeying through life. I am using the word *aspects* in order to suggest that these are not strict chronological stages. Every woman is multifaceted, having many defining characteristics at once. However, the developmental view suggests that at every point in our lives we see ourselves as having one aspect more dominant than another. A woman can be a young woman, a mother, and a widow at the same time, but the important reality is how she sees herself. Does she see herself as a young woman, a mother, or a widow? Which aspect of her personhood will be the controlling or defining characteristic?

So these various stages of a woman's life are more logical seasons or aspects than strict chronological ones. Don't worry about the order. Try to identify with the defining characteristics and feelings of each stage. The stages are not meant to be prescriptive in any way. The last thing I want to do is to tell other women what I think they *should* experience. In this book I am merely describing what I believe to be the longstanding biblical observations about the various normative experiences in women's lives. I think as we compare our lives today with the women and the terms used to describe women in the Scriptures, we will find an amazing compatibility. The nature of women has not changed, nor have the experiences they have faced over the thousands of years of human history.

## SIX ASPECTS OF A WOMAN'S LIFE

The characteristics or aspects of a woman's life that we will study are derived from the distinct Hebrew and Greek terms used in the Scriptures for "woman." Starting with the Creational Woman (*'Adam*/Eve), we will discover the identity that is ours by design and what we have lost as a result of sin entering into the world. In chapter 3 we will focus on the Young Woman (*neqevah* and *parthenos*), discussing the power the young woman has in her beauty, in both its proper and improper expression. We will look at what influences have created a sexual fantasy world for both women and men and the resulting problems. The conclusion demonstrates the striking realization that both sexes have worshiped at the altar of beauty.

The Nurturing Woman (*em* and *mater*) illustrates the unique nurturing side of a woman that she brings into every area of life. Today, when the value and credibility of motherhood has been challenged by the feminist movement, what intrinsic aspect of nurturing has been lost or denied by the challenge? Nurturing is so vital within family relationships, but its impact is also felt in the workplace, church, and other relationships and activities. Nurturing one's self is also vitally important. Some women have trouble doing this due to the neglect of early nurturing by their own mothers, or the pain of dysfunctional family backgrounds, divorce, abuse, and other problems.

The Relational Woman (*'ishsah* and *gune*) defines the core of a woman's personhood. Women are defined as often by their relationships as men are defined by their vocations. The relational woman has a desire for intimacy. She also desires to have an impact through her relationships as expressed in her family, workplace, and world. This relational orientation, however, can lead to many disappointments and difficult adjustments with her male counterpart. A healthy knowledge and acceptance of gender differences enhance this stop on her journey.

Ultimately we will see that the woman's relationship with her Creator will bring her peace with the other relationships in her life.

The Wounded Woman (*'enosh, almanah, chera*) is a normal but painful phase of the woman's journey. Unmet needs, broken relationships, unexpected tragic events, and the daily grind can leave many women bleeding and unattended alongside the road. A woman at this stage needs to claim her woundedness, reframe it in a positive light, and discover a new meaning for her life. This renewal can bring healing to the wounds and keep her moving forward on the path. Her wounds may even become her greatest altar of contribution if she will not allow herself to "waste her sorrows."

The woman wounded by the loss of her most significant relationships is studied using the term *widow* (*almanah* and *chera*). This period is a road most women will eventually find themselves on as they complete their journey. Some experience this phase of life sooner than others. This is a difficult time, and one that requires special attention, honor, and care from others. The time of loss, grief, aloneness, and challenging responsibilities can be overwhelming for many.

The ancient Scriptures are clear on the position of widows and God's love toward them. The potential for stagnation is great at this fork in the road, but the options for service and usefulness are many. The choice is individual. Prudent decisions here carve out a new pathway toward wisdom during the twilight years.

The Strong Woman (*'eshet hayil*) is the final stop on this earthly journey. It is here that the mature qualities of womanhood are seen. Younger women should desire these qualities and pursue them, yet few seem to do either. This "excellent" woman is a strong woman, having worth, recognition, and strength of character. But these are seen only as she looks back. Her hope, encouragement, and experiences from life mentor her younger sisters as they grow toward the future.

In this sense, she is a pioneer, one who has gone ahead and marked the path that others may follow. Her portrait is found in the wisdom literature and stands as a voice calling to the younger women of any generation. Her contribution is great, and the praises that come to her from others make her journey worthwhile.

## HOW CAN TWO WRITE ONE BOOK?

Very painfully! If you haven't noticed by now, there are two names on the cover—Cynthia Hicks (that's me) and Robert Hicks (that's my husband). Since he wrote *The Masculine Journey*, and this book complements his work, we thought it would be reasonable for us to do this one together. But as usual, what sounds easy in the "thinking" stage can be far from easy in the "doing" stage. Someone must make decisions about style, word choice, grammar, tense, and so on. So, as you read through the pages of this book, keep in mind that the "I" is me—Cinny, my nickname for Cynthia.

However, throughout the process of writing, both of us were involved. Bob would write a section and I would edit, critique, argue, and rewrite. Then I would write a section and Bob would edit, critique, argue, and rewrite. Most of the historical background, language studies, and technical data is Bob's contribution. The experiences alluded to are obviously my own. The result of the writing process and interaction is, of course, a book in the feminine voice, a feminine journey.

As I look back on my journey thus far, I wish I could have known when I started out that many of the things I wrote about in this book were normal developmental aspects of a woman's life. Perhaps I wouldn't have thought I was going crazy or that other women had it all together when I didn't. Perhaps I would have had a more realistic view of life, marriage, parenting, and my Christian walk. Maybe I would have known God still loved me when I crawled into my cave of woundedness.

My hope for this book is that sharing my journey will encourage you, my sisters, to cut yourselves a little slack, to enjoy the pleasant scenery at every stage, and to realize you are normal and not alone.

As I try to look ahead on my journey, it is still scary at times. No one really knows what is ahead. That's why Abraham was so commended for his faith when "he went out, not knowing where he was going" (Hebrews 11:8). But at least I know I should expect change and not be bound to the way I think the trip should go.

Between our own desires and the delights and deceptions of this earth, we can get detoured and lost very easily. Our journey is not one that is our own design, but one that comes from above. The Architect and Builder of our lives is God. He is the Creator, and we are the creatures. But being creational means some very unique things for a woman. Our journey begins by understanding what it means to be made in God's image as a creational woman.

# CHAPTER TWO

# CREATIONAL WOMAN:
# A WOMAN OF CONTRARY APPETITES

*Of two evils, choose the prettier.*
CAROLYN WELLS

*There is no animal more invincible than a woman,*
*nor fire either, nor any wildcat so ruthless.*
ARISTOPHANES

We were the Winter Park Wildcats of Winter Park, Florida. The graduating class of 1965. Our yearbook was the *Towayam*. I've hung on to my high school year books for almost thirty years. Through all the moves and across all the miles, I carted those books around.

One summer morning, while cleaning the attic to make room for our daughter's high school stuff before she went off to college, I stumbled across my neglected yearbooks. With cup of coffee in hand, I settled down to an unplanned walk along memory lane.

## YEARBOOK IDENTITY

Many people I know don't want to have another thought about high school. The reason is simple: Those weren't the best of years for them. Those years may have been a painful time in the process of adolescent development. Therefore, the last thing a person may want to do is to relive the pain of loneliness, academic struggle, too little popularity, romantic failures, or total disgust with one's body, skin, and hair.

For others, like me, those were the best of years! In high school our identity, ambitions, and dreams dominated our thoughts—when they weren't on boys, that is! For many of us, the friends we laughed with, cried with, and shared our most intimate secrets with were the

29

best friends we thought we would ever have. What was it about those years that made the bonds so tight?

For me, Winter Park High School was as good as it gets! The discovery of my yearbook that day turned into hours as I reminisced about the good ol' days. I laughed at the pictures and remembered the special events caught by the school photographer. What really held my thoughts were the personal comments written in the yearbook by my friends and those I worshiped from afar. In that moment, I felt the same warm, hopeful, emotional feelings I experienced when I first read them. I quickly and excitedly identified with that very optimistic, energetic, in-shape eighteen-year-old who thought she knew who she was and what she wanted out of life.

We had a section in the *Towayam* for outstanding seniors. Imagine my excitement when I saw my picture and this paragraph in that special section of the yearbook:

CINNY BLISS . . . Cinny Bliss, who is one of WPHS's future civic leaders, headed the Winter Park Youth Center Youth Council this year among other achievements. A student council representative for two years and a member of Tri-Hi-Y for three, Cinny was secretary of the Senior Class this year. A dependable and enthusiastic worker, Cinny served on the Prom and Christmas Formal Committees.

Whether we realize it or not, a great deal of our self-perception in high school is derived from the opinions of others, particularly from those we admire. As I read the comments written by my friends, I was amazed by their perspective of who I was. I felt gratitude for their generosity and love. The esteem I had derived from my high school years made the transition to college more bearable. My first year of college was lonely and difficult. During that time, I just kept remembering who I really was and from where I had come.

Many years have passed since the simple, carefree, fun-filled, self-centered days of youth. Turbulent cultural changes from the late sixties to the nineties, along with the demands of adulthood, marriage, and children, have left that naive, confident, wide-eyed girl lost in a feminine maze. The introspective sixties caused all baby boomers to ask, Who am I? and What am I supposed to do with my life?

As a girl raised in the South, I had approached adulthood with all the traditional views of being a wife and mother. Career options were still narrow for most women in college. Education was viewed as an end in itself, but the process of education was not valued in terms other than helping a woman find a "good" husband or giving her something to fall back on should the "good" husband lose his job or die (or these days, divorce you).

I found the "good" husband and married right out of college, had three children and found myself too busy with diapers, dishes, and wifely duties to have the time or energy to think about who I was.

A few years ago, as life calmed down and the children grew up, I began to notice in my daughters' lives different paths than the one I had followed. I woke up as if from a dream and found that the structure of the traditional woman's role I had known and placed so much value in had virtually collapsed. I observed that the traditional woman's role appeared to be in total conflict with the new feminist philosophy. However, today from my mid-life perspective, I find women struggling in both camps. Feminists are going back home to have kids.

One serious career woman, journalist Linda Ellerby, made the following comment in a recent television interview as she looked back on her years as a mother: "If I had to do it all over again, I would have told the networks no and stayed home with my children more often." She went on to say, "Corporations don't always keep score, but children do."[1] She tried to combine family and career but felt she didn't do it very well!

There are many "working moms" who don't necessarily identify with the feminist movement or agenda, but have to work to help finance their mortgages or support their children as single moms. It seems like the feminist and traditional models for women are unrealistic and failing. Most women live somewhere between these two conflicting models of womanhood. Some illustrations may be helpful at this point.

Susan is a TV anchor woman and the mother of two small boys. She started in the broadcast industry almost fifteen years ago. Through hard work and persistence, she moved from being a weekend sports reporter to being the co-anchor of the nightly news. Being a woman in the male-dominated news and television business has been a challenge for her. But Susan is an articulate, intelligent, persistent woman who has climbed this tall ladder, yet maintained her femininity, her faith, and her family. Her two sons are her top priority, along with her husband.

Susan is successful in her career and does not identify with the feminist agenda, although she would agree with the issues of equal rights and equal pay for women in the marketplace. She continues to maintain her Christian values and believes she is fulfilling her responsibilities as a wife and mother. As a mother who works outside of the home, Susan relies on a wonderful helper for her children. She has found that working and being a parent is much tougher than when she worked but had no children. However, the children come before her career.

It's not easy juggling both worlds. It takes patience, realistic expectations, a sense of humor, and being constantly reminded of priorities. The tensions for a working mother (whether at home or elsewhere) are simply a reality and can cause stress and exhaustion. However, she believes she can contribute to the well-being of her family both financially and emotionally by being at home.

Cathy now finds herself a working woman after being a "stay-at-home" wife and mom for fifteen years. During the last three years, economic demands including the desire to send four children to college have pushed Cathy out of the home into the workplace. She juggles a full-time teaching position in a junior high school with the demands of going home to three children every evening. Her oldest daughter is in her first year of college.

Although Cathy's husband has a good job, this couple, like so many today, can no longer meet their financial obligations without the wife working. From September through May she is exhausted from trying to balance a full-time job with full-time motherhood. Having had those years at home with the first two children, she feels guilty about not being there for the last two in the same way. However, she says, "I've enjoyed the benefits—the accomplishment and achievement—my work provides. Parenting is just more difficult since I've started teaching."

These examples of mothers with careers are not unique. Today over half of American women are in the work force, up from 27 percent in 1940.[2] Even among those committed to the traditional model where women should not work outside the home, there seems to be some fudging. Bob once met with a group who believed very strongly that a women's place was at home with her kids. Over 90 percent of the audience raised their hands to affirm such. But then he asked, "How many of you or your wives are currently doing something 'at home' to realize additional income?" About 80 percent of the group raised their hands!

Women are not in the traditional roles of wife and mother as known in the fifties or early sixties. But this change does not negate their commitment to the traditional values of parenting and marriage. It would seem the traditional role for women as we have known it is no longer the norm. The impact of the women's movement and economic survival issues have created new options and tensions for women. The issues the feminist movement has raised are complex, and in some way have touched all our lives.

*Megatrends for Women*, a book that targets the trends caused by the effects of the women's movement and tracks the paths of the "liberated woman," has become a best-selling volume. The authors, Patricia Aburdene and John Naisbitt, say that their book is "about powerful women transforming an imperfect world."[3] They write that women are exerting their power and "are transforming the different arenas [every aspect of life] . . . by building a new reality, a new social order or paradigm that will eventually replace the old order based on the domination of the male sex, its values and power."[4]

The authors believe the world is suddenly a woman's oyster; everything lies at our feet today. We are told that there are no differences between men and women and that we can have it all. Many women today make individual choices within a value system of expediency rather than truth.

There is something healthy about choice. It implies that you are thinking and taking a conscious responsibility for your life rather than performing your role in an unconscious, rote fashion. What is critical is the reference point upon which the choices are made. This journey of life is bumpy and up for grabs, as the maps keep changing.

Looking at the multiple options for women today, I wasn't sure which path I was to follow on my feminine journey. As much as I loved what I read in my yearbook, those perspectives of who I was then were gleaned from other naive youth (who probably didn't know who they really were either!). I needed to go farther back in time in order to trace more truthfully the beginning of my feminine journey.

## BIBLICAL IDENTITY FOR WOMEN

I believe in a Creator who designed women for a uniquely different kind of journey than that of men. In creating the human species, He created them male and female (Genesis 1:27). In other words, there are two ways of being human—maleness and femaleness.

But the voices of the feminist movement, in fighting a battle for sexual equality, have either consciously or unconsciously tried to affirm that there are no real differences between men and women. Even though the fight has been political, the feminist impact on women's issues has permeated every aspect of life, from the bedroom to the boardroom to the courtroom. But changing laws and attitudes do not change human nature. Even in the civil rights arena, do women merely want to walk in a man's footsteps, sharing equally *his* rights, privileges, and responsibilities? In reading some of the feminist material, it seems they are seeking to become men, not be women.

Some traditionalists claim women were created to be subservient to men and, in fact, created for his good pleasure. Is this really the only purpose for women? Dr. James Dobson has written that low self-esteem is the major problem for women today. Where does the lack of self-esteem—self-contempt—originate?

Nancy Groom writes in *From Bondage to Bonding* that self-contempt "is an expression of the belief that one's personhood is hopelessly flawed and unchangeable."[5] This self-degradation perpetuates the idea of being a victim, feeling powerless and worthless. Never before have women had more self-help books and more maps to assist them on their journey of self-exploration. But it seems that the deeper women dig, the bigger the hole, and they are left as confused as ever.

The women of North America are more than willing to air their complaints, struggles, and woundedness on endless television talk shows in a candor foreign to the last generation. But if they are in some way looking for a greater sense of self, where does the concept of self-esteem originate? Why do men and women assume that self-esteem is a positive attribute anyway? Is it something a person can conjure up within herself through positive self-talk, as many motivational books and speakers proclaim? These unanswered questions drove me back to where the Bible begins. I realized that ultimately the creation must consult the Creator. Women must seek understanding for their identity at the source, at the beginning not only of their personal journey but of the journey for all mankind.

## THE CREATIONAL WOMAN

The first stage of the feminine journey is shared with our male counterpart. God made both sexes in His own image. The term the biblical writers used to describe this image is the Hebrew word *'adam*.[6] In

Genesis 1:26-27 we read, "Then God said, 'Let Us make man in Our image, according to Our likeness; . . .' And God created man [*'adam*] in His own image, in the image of God He created him; male and female He created them."

The first chapter of Genesis is a summary statement about the creation, which is typical of Hebrew writing. Genesis 1 outlines the divisions between light and darkness, the creation of the earth and heavens, the division between day and night, the creation of all living creatures in the air and the water and on land.

On the sixth day God produced His *"pièce de résistance"* and created man in the form of male and female. He then extended His grace in the form of a blessing, an unconditional benediction not given to any other part of the creation (1:28). Man was set apart from the rest of creation. Mankind was special. "God saw all that He had made, and behold it was very good" (1:31). And God rested!

Genesis 2 is more specific as it gives the chronological details of the creation events, including human beings. As a skilled Craftsman, God fashions the body of the male out of the dust of the earth. The Hebrew word *'adam* is given by the Creator to this human species, which conveys the idea of "dark, red soil and red blood." As the prophet Isaiah will later say, "Thou art our Father, we are the clay and Thou our potter; and all of us are the work of Thy hand" (64:8).

God formed man and "breathed into his nostrils the breath of life; and man [*'adam*] became a living being" (Genesis 2:7).

Matthew Henry states,

Let the soul which God has breathed into us, breathe after Him; and let it be for Him, since it is from Him. Into His hands let us commit our spirits, for from His hands we had them. It takes its lodging in a house of clay and is the life and support of it. It is by it that man is a living soul, that is, a living man; for the soul is the man. The body would be a worthless, useless, loathsome carcass, if the soul did not animate it.[7]

This rational, immortal soul of man was given by God to live in a relationship with Him in a paradise designed by God for man's happiness.

Women are, in general, more aware of and particular about their surroundings than their male counterparts. The grandeur of the garden that God planted for man was beyond man's imagination: "Out of the ground the LORD God caused to grow every tree that is pleasing to the sight and good for food" (2:9). Rivers flowed throughout and gold laced the landscape. The garden was named "Eden," which signifies delight and pleasure.

God put man into the Garden of Eden to cultivate it and keep it. He pointed out two particular trees to Adam, the tree of life and the tree of the knowledge of good and evil. Adam's responsibility was to serve and take care of the garden God had given him and to guard and protect it. God instructed Adam that he was free to eat the fruit of any of the trees except one, the tree of the knowledge of good and evil. God's authority was clear and this doesn't sound like an unreasonable command. Adam had complete dominion with only one prohibition.

In the next event during creation, we get a peek into God's awareness of Adam's need and the creative way in which it was awakened. God said, "It is not good for the man to be alone; I will make him a helper suitable for him" (2:18). God is a relational being and imparted to Adam this same relational nature. Through the process of naming the animals as God created them, Adam became aware that none of them were like him. And each animal had a mate except Adam: "There was not found a helper suitable for him" (2:20). Adam may have pondered this observation and then did what all men do after a hard day's work: he fell asleep.

God alone knows what will satisfy His creation. He took a rib from Adam and fashioned it into a woman. He then brought man's counterpart to him. Perhaps this was a subtle way of letting mankind know that gaining a partner will always cost something. Imagine Adam's surprise upon waking and seeing this creature. He said, "This is now bone of my bones, and flesh of my flesh; she shall be called Woman, because she was taken out of man." In other words, his response was "*Wow!* Where have you been all my life?!"

Adam called her "woman," which is the Hebrew word *'ishah*. This word is the same as his name *'ish*, only with a feminine ending. He acknowledged that she was like him, but also different in being female. Going back to Genesis 1, we are reminded that God blessed them both and gave them the commands of reproduction and rulership.

In God's fashioning of the woman, He stated that she would be a "helper, suitable for man." This has been interpreted by some as giving a woman an inferior position to a man; she was created merely to serve him. However, the Hebrew term for "helper" is *'ezer*. It implies divine aid or assistance as is often used in the book of Psalms: "God is our refuge and strength; a very present *help* in trouble" (46:1, emphasis added). Many other passages that convey the idea of God's divine aid on behalf of His people include the word *'ezer*.

The woman is uniquely made for the man. God did not find man's aloneness to be good. In response, He did not seek to satisfy this male species with something from the animal world. Neither did He meet man's need of a helper through another man. As the bumper stickers proclaim, God fashioned Eve, not Steve! God created a human being like *'adam*, but also different to fill the gaps. The old saying that "opposites attract" finds its reality here. As confusing as it may seem, men and women come together in their diversity and find completeness and unity.

Creational woman, by design, is a coequal with her man. They are, of course, vastly different in body structure, but have the same responsibilities and dignity. It is through their coming together that their diversity in unity reflects more fully the image of God. The man and his wife are anatomically different, yet physically compatible. Their coming together forms a unique unity. It is for this cause of unity and its priority over all other relationships that the man is instructed to leave his parents and unite with his wife, that they may become one. This oneness will be reflected not only in their relationship but in their offspring. The beauty, honesty, and innocence of this relationship is revealed in the phrase *they were both naked and were not ashamed.*

## Woman of Dignity

It is here, in the first two chapters of the Bible, that the rationale for women's self-esteem is found. The word *esteem* means to "regard favorably; to respect; to prize" according to the dictionary. It means to have dignity by design. This dignity and worth are not the result of a woman's own efforts or accomplishments. A woman is not valuable because of her marriage, her children, or her career. These can all be important parts of a woman's life, but they are not the reasons for her personal dignity.

The woman was created in the image of God and set apart from the rest of creation. God blessed her and called her very good. This is where a woman derives her esteem and dignity. In ancient days, the image of a ruler was imprinted on coins to signify his authority and thus gain allegiance from his people. God has left His mark on His image, man, in the male and female relationship, which illustrates in a limited way His divine attributes. For a woman to fight for or search for dignity and affirmation apart from her association with the Divine

Creator is meaningless. A woman's intrinsic value is a result of God's stamp on her as His unique creation.

Living in a results and performance-oriented world makes it very difficult to grasp the concept of intrinsic dignity and esteem. To understand that God loves me just because He made me—with no strings attached—is amazing. No, it's completely irrational! Unconditional love is so foreign to the natural mind. Human relationships have so many requirements, demands, and conditions that blur and hinder the expression of this truth. As children we learn very early to please our parents or suffer the consequences. In school, children are regularly graded on their academic performance, which deeply affirms or scars their self-image. In the world of business, size of paychecks, job promotions, or being fired continue to perpetuate the reality that one is only as good as one's performance. As one woman told me, "She was only as good as her last success!"

Is it any wonder that we find it so difficult, if not impossible, to accept the concept of human value merely for the sake of being! A male friend of ours is a living model of what it means to have intrinsic value and to feel valued just for being who he is, without any performance requirements.

Dennis was a member of a singing group, The New Folk (now The Old Folk!), in which Bob and I traveled over twenty years ago. Dennis had a powerful personality and was the spokesperson for the group as we sang and shared the Christian message with college students around the country. During the year we traveled with him Dennis was diagnosed as having multiple sclerosis. This was a radical change of direction for Dennis on his life journey.

We kept in touch with Dennis and watched from a distance as the disease progressively claimed his body but never his spirit. Several years ago, Dennis came to live with our family for over six months. Dennis never saw himself as a victim of life, nor became bitter or full of self-pity. He accepted the painful detour on his journey. Dennis conquered the death of many dreams, ambitions, and relationships, as well as the loss of his leg. His countenance was always one of quiet, peaceful dignity.

Dennis observed my racing around, my perfectionistic tendencies, and my dissatisfaction about so many areas. He reminded me, by his words and his presence, that God loved me just the way I was. Dennis could not do any of those things that I felt were so important. He used to say, "Cinny, if I were confined to my bed and could never get up again to do anything, would God love me any less? You see, He loves me just because I'm His." I used to think that I was the handicapped one, not Dennis.

I agree with the feminists' pursuit of equal opportunities for women in the workplace. However, as noted earlier, even Gloria Steinem admitted that equal rights cannot guarantee self-esteem. A woman finding her value in her work, career, or performance is just as fragile as a man finding his worth there. One may do fine until she is out of work, her performance is marginal, or her husband leaves. Until a woman accepts the self-esteem that she already has by being a unique creation of God, her identity is tenuous.

The first realization every woman must face on this feminine journey is that she is creational; her worth is to be found in what she already is. Self-esteem is not something to be sought, but something to be discovered as already there.

### Woman of Responsibility: Reproduce and Rule

God created the perfect environment for the perfect couple! To reproduce and rule were responsibilities given equally to the female as well as the male. There was no apparent conflict in the responsibilities, as both brought their unique abilities to the tasks. The task of reproduction is one of pleasure and of procuring the continuance of humankind. The physical coming together in intercourse illustrates the creational differences in their bodies.

Through this reproductive act women in particular come into an awareness of their maternal and nurturing natures. To many women is granted the privilege of bearing children. In chapter 4, "The Nurturer," we will discuss this unique aspect of women.

For those of you who are single or do not have children, portions of that chapter will not be relevant to you or may even cause some pain. However, a portion of "The Nurturer" deals with the nurturing aspect of women as applicable in their careers and relationships. The woundedness of childlessness will be addressed in chapter 6, "The Wounded Woman," and I hope will ease any pain or deep regret you may feel.

In the past few decades, women have been encouraged to give more priority to their own rights than to those of their unborn children or to the rights of the father. Abortion is an action that seems to separate women from their nurturing natures and thus from their own femininity. Does the pro-choice option really give women the right to exercise their femaleness, or has it, in reality, resulted in separating them from it?

Not too long ago I was invited to attend a convention at which only women were promoting their businesses. The theme of the day was "Women Doing Business with Women." I leisurely strolled from booth to booth chatting with women, looking at their products and services offered to other women in the community. I happened upon a booth representing a political candidate. A couple stood behind the table handing out booklets and other written information. I stopped to talk to the man, surprised to see a male at this event. Our conversation took us to the campaign issues addressed by his candidate.

The man said, "You should seriously consider, as a woman, voting for our candidate because of her strong pro-choice position on abortion."

I replied, "It is because I am a woman that I do not support the pro-choice position. I support the issue of life and defending the rights of the unborn child."

The man seemed taken by surprise and responded, "Certainly you support a woman's right to decide what to do with her own body. After all, it is her body."

I found myself reacting emotionally to this man telling me, a woman, how I should feel about the subject. As I handed the material back to him, I said, "My body has been designed to give life, which I have done on three occasions. It is not my desire to turn this life-giving ability into an instrument of destruction of my own child."

How far away from the original design have women fallen! This is not a treatise on pro-life versus pro-choice, but I do support the right of life over the right of choice. This is not to say that there aren't times—the exception and not the rule—when tough decisions about the life of the mother over the child have to be made. However, this is not always the issue in the thousands of abortions performed daily. In my opinion, the pro-choice movement has done more to damage the dignity of women than any other single issue in our country.

Mother Teresa, a Nobel peace prize winner, who fights so desperately for the dignity of the dying, was interviewed a few years ago. In the interview she commented about the mass destruction of children in North America. Her response was that America should send its unwanted children to her. Despite the poverty and death of her surroundings, she said they would find a way to take care of the children that the selfish, materialistic West did not want.

What an indictment upon our value system and view of life. If women and mothers will not fight for their children, who will? There is no hope. Women have abdicated this God-given responsibility and will be held accountable.

In addition to reproduction, both the woman and the man were given rulership or stewardship over God's creation. For many centuries, it seems we have lived under an unconscious delusion that the world is ours to use and abuse. We have come to realize our earth does not contain limitless resources. Efforts are now being made to be more environmentally aware. The irony is that it is more sophisticated and popular to be concerned with saving whales and other endangered species than with saving our unborn children. They are the truly endangered species today on American soil!

In this industrial and technological age we have alienated ourselves from the earth. Many people live in concrete jungles without a blade of grass or a single tree. No wonder the level of violence is so intense in these overpopulated, concrete ghettos. The people have no place to go to clear their heads. Children have no parks to play in, and end up on the streets.

This brings to mind the movie *The Women of Brewster Place*. It conveyed the plight of black women trapped in concrete slums. The end of their street is blocked off, separating them from the rest of the city. The brick wall symbolizes their ostracism and hopeless separation from any upward mobility to improve their lives. The movie portrays the difficulties of black ghetto women, their struggle to survive, and the strength of their relational bonds. The movie ends with these women tearing the brick wall down with their bare hands as a symbol of breaking free from the entrapment they experience.

When life, activities, and problems press in on me, I find tremendous peace and refuge in the outdoors. I am more fortunate than the women of Brewster Place because I have been blessed with wonderful places to which I can escape. My mother has a home in Blowing Rock, North Carolina. Occasionally I have the opportunity to visit her. My favorite place is on her deck overlooking the Blue Ridge Mountains. I love to sit and gaze at the lush, green landscape that is capped off by the mountains in the distance. There is a certain tranquility and peace in the sound of the wind moving through the trees. Overhead I can listen to the sound of the rapid beating of a hummingbird's wings. In that serene setting, life makes more sense. Problems don't seem so insurmountable, and my perspective becomes clearer.

When we take the time to listen to the sounds of nature, or put our hands in rich soil to plant bulbs or flowers, we just seem to feel better. Maybe there is a parallel here. As we get more in touch with our natural world, we also get more in touch with ourselves! We were made from the dust, and it feels comfortable, like coming home, to reconnect for a brief moment. Because I was raised in Florida and lived in Hawaii for several years, I am most deeply affected by the ocean. My favorite time to enjoy the beach is early in the morning. The feel of the cool breeze across the water, the waves licking the shore time after time, the clean, unmarked sand, and the vast expanse of the water all seem to be very therapeutic. It brings healing to my soul. Creation is our garden, and we need to serve and protect it, both for our own enjoyment and for the enjoyment of our posterity.

**Woman of Fallibility**

We left Adam and his wife in paradise, tending their garden, naked and unashamed. The Hebrew term for naked is *'arummin*, which implies vulnerability and innocence. In Genesis 3, a new character is introduced, unannounced and unexplained . . . the serpent. We are told this longstanding representation of evil is cunning. The Hebrew word for cunning or shrewd is *'arum*. Classic Hebrew poetry takes two words that sound similar and connects them to form a theological concept. The words *'arum* (cunning or shrewd) and *'arummin* (naked) sound similar but are in direct contrast in meaning.

Here we have a subtle play on words in order to make a profound connection between the vulnerability of the couple and the craftiness of the serpent. The serpent focuses his attention on the unique vulnerability of the couple. The subtle Hebrew connection increases the sense of naive vulnerability in the couple and the utter terror that is suggested by the craftiness of the serpent.

Where as Adam was the focal point up to now, in Genesis 3 the woman now takes center stage. She is the one approached by the serpent. This shrewd antagonist seems to appear out of nowhere, waiting for the right time to do his damage.

Who was this serpent? He was obviously different from the other animals because he had the power of speech and reasoning. We are told that "he was more crafty than any other beast of the field which the LORD God had made." But this implies that he was one of the creation over which the couple should rule. They had a God-ordained right to rule him!

The serpent directs his comments to the woman. He challenges God's clear commands about eating from the trees in the garden and then questions the one prohibition that God had placed upon the couple. The serpent brings into question the character of God by questioning His reason for forbidding the couple to eat of this one tree: "If God is really good, then shouldn't He want you to eat of everything He has created?"

**Woman's Vulnerability: Dissatisfaction**
The serpent, of course is lying in his explanation of God's motives and interpretation of God's character. (Only God can explain His own motives for doing things!) But the serpent does raise serious doubts in the woman's mind. She had never questioned God before or thought to argue or disagree with any command He had given. Suddenly, the serpent plants a seed of dissatisfaction in the woman's mind. He causes her to focus, not on the glorious and plentiful creation God had given them to enjoy, but on the one tree that had been prohibited.

Lust is born in deception and gives birth to feminine dissatisfaction. The woman's eye now sees the forbidden tree in a new perspective. Magically transformed by the power of words (compare this with modern advertising), the tree looked like it had fruit too wonderful to pass up. It was a delight to her eye, and she desired to eat of its wisdom above all else.

Does this sound familiar? A woman can be totally at peace with her home until she picks up the latest edition of *House Beautiful*. Immediately she looks at her home and wants to redecorate. Maybe you find your mailbox overflowing with those enticing catalogs full of items you never knew existed. But instantly, you can't live without them! A personal confession comes to mind of an incident that robbed me of peace for months.

I was home minding my own business, cleaning and feeling pretty good about the end results. I had dusted, mopped, straightened, and vacuumed. Things were shining! Then there was a knock at the door. Was it my neighbor? I answered and found a man standing there with a lot of equipment in hand. He was a vacuum cleaner salesman. He had just been at my neighbor's house, and of course she had said she loved his product and knew I would feel the same way. He wanted to come in and show me how it worked.

He was a persuasive talker and before I knew it, he was putting his machine together. I told him my carpets were clean as I had just vacuumed. At that point, he turned his machine on and away he went. The dirt and stuff that he pulled out of my carpet was shocking and embarrassing. Imagine, all this time I had been satisfied with my little, apparently very inadequate, vacuum cleaner.

Next came the sales pitch. He said, "You do love your family, don't you?"

I said, "Well of course I do."

He went on. "Then how can you not want them to live in the very cleanest house possible?"

I just stood there with my mouth open.

He continued. "You are obviously a very particular woman with excellent taste. This machine is the very best there is and you certainly do deserve to have it."

Well, I couldn't argue with that. My only question was, "How much does it cost?"

This crafty salesman said, "It doesn't cost much and is worth every penny. Wouldn't you agree?"

I said, "Yes."

"Great," he said, as he got out his book and started writing. "How do you want to pay for this—check or charge?"

I knew there wasn't enough money in the checking account, and Bob would be furious if I charged it. I said I would have to wait and talk to my husband about this.

The salesman made a gallant attempt to close the deal. He could see that the vacuum cleaner had caught my eye, and he was right. I was now totally dissatisfied with my present machine, so I told him I would figure out a way to pay for it. The man left, and I spent the rest of the day trying to figure out how I could come up with the money to buy this marvelous machine.

Bob came home, listened to the story, and heard my plea. He said he was sure it was a great machine, but we just didn't need it. (Typical male response!) Of course he didn't think we needed it. He hadn't seen what it could do.

The salesman kept calling, and I kept trying to find a way to buy this machine. Over a period of weeks, however, the memory of the machine's performance began to fade, but the reality of our financial position stayed the same. I finally told the salesman on his fourth call, "Look, I know this is the top-of-the-line vacuum and I would love to have it. The truth is, I don't own the top of the line of anything and I guess we won't start here. Thanks, but no thanks."

The truth was that at this point I was very agitated over the entire situation. I was frustrated with my *need* to have this machine and wanted my peace back. I was angry at the man for disrupting my peace and ruining what little thrill I had over the performance of my own vacuum. I decided that contentment takes a lot less energy than dissatisfaction, and results in far more peace.

The issue that my sister in the garden faced was by no means as trivial as mine. However, her dissatisfaction created havoc and a disruption that would affect humanity for all time, even you and me. As a result of this original deception, I believe we as women have continued to be vulnerable in the area of dissatisfaction.

Thanks to the "great American fantasy machine" and the entire advertising industry, women are kept dissatisfied on their feminine journey. Women today are bombarded by false images of what they are supposed to want and need in every area of their life. Television, soap operas, and movies portray a fantasy life of romance, wealth, and beauty. The world of advertising plays on this fantasy and creates inordinate desires that breed dissatisfaction and discontent for one's lot.

For some women, the lust of the eyes has resulted in adultery, serious debts, the destruction of families, the infection of sexually transmitted diseases, even death. The serpent of this world still seduces us where we are the most vulnerable. What looked so beautiful and so desirable in the beginning ends up being ugly, painful, and not worth the price.

As women, we need to embrace seriously the reality encouraged by the Apostle John:

> Do not love the world, nor the things in the world. . . . For all that is in the world, the lust of the flesh and the lust of the eyes and the boastful pride of life, is not from the Father but is from the world. (1 John 2:15-16)

The serpent deceived the woman and she ate the forbidden fruit. Not only did she eat, but "she gave it to her husband with her and he ate." Yes, he had been there all the time. Adam's lack of intervention into this disobedient action brought him into the corruption as well.

The question of the ages is of course, Why didn't Adam step in before it was too late? It was to Adam personally that God gave the commandment about the tree in the midst of the garden. Whether He gave this command again to Eve, or Adam told her, we don't know.

But the point is, they both knew exactly what God said.

Adam's lack of intervention is no speculation, but the reason is open to speculation. One thought is that he was so captivated with the beauty of his wife that he lost his perspective on his divine accountability. The power of a woman's beauty has over a man is not only strong, but rarely understood. It overshadows rational thinking among men every day. The results are disastrous for both women and men. Larry Crabb wrote in *Men and Women: Enjoying the Differences*,

> Adam shifted his allegiance away from God to Eve, and Eve shifted her allegiance away from God and his design for her to the giver of the forbidden fruit.
> Thus, Adam and Eve's standing naked before God exposed something ugly about their sexual identity as man and woman, their sinfulness extended into the deepest parts of their beings. If at core they are male and female, persons with distinctive sexual identities, then their masculinity and femininity were deeply involved in the corruption.[8]

This disobedient act results in the loss of innocence for all time. Adam and his wife immediately see each other in a fallen light and realize they are naked. The Hebrew word *'arrumin*, meaning "naked," is always used as a negative exposure (except in Genesis 2). The innocence of their nakedness is gone forever and replaced with the experience of shame. Shame now enters into the core of human personhood.

Shame implies a sense of being deceived or duped by a third party. In man's fallenness, men and women feel victimized. There is a sense that something precious has been taken from them. In the garden, this first couple could no longer face God. Theological shame now separated the once intimate relationship between the couple and their Creator. Their attempts to hide from God and cover their nakedness only illustrate their newfound shame.

Women and men have continued in endless, futile attempts to cover their shortcomings from each other and from God. Feelings of inadequacy and inferiority are hidden within the human heart.

## WOMEN HIDE THEIR SHAME

Every religion in the world has some provision or means by which its gods can be appeased. There seems to be some innate awareness in humans of this need to make atonement. Some believe that through humanitarian social involvement or religious activity they might be able to cover the inner shame. Some have despaired and given up. Others try to rationalize away their inner shame and guilt by ignoring God altogether.

However man tries to hide from God and his own shame, there is still a seeking God who continues to reach out to His creation. God haunts us with the message of His Son, who is the only cure for the inner shame we feel before Him.

The cover-up before God fails. He finds the couple hiding in their shame and addresses Adam first. Adam accepts no responsibility for his disobedience, but instantly blames the one given to him as his unique counterpart: "The woman whom Thou gavest to be with me, she gave me from the tree and I ate." The woman responds in kind, by blaming another: "The serpent deceived me and I ate." Neither one assumes personal responsibility. Like children, they shift the blame around the circle of participants, each for fear of his or her own judgment.

Finally, the serpent is cursed by God and told of his ultimate destruction. He is the only recipient of God's curse. God never curses what He has already blessed, even when there is extreme failure![9]

God's judgment upon the woman lies in two areas. First, she is told that she will experience increased pain in childbearing. You mothers reading this will testify to the pain of childbirth. I found it an experiential reality three times. However, every time I went through it, the memory of the pain diminished with time and I found myself wanting to go through it once more. The joy of holding a radiant newborn far outweighs the temporary feelings of discomfort.

Having been a mother for twenty-some years now, it seems that childbirth was the easiest phase of motherhood. The pains experienced in the process of parenting far outweigh the momentary physical pain at the beginning. Ask any parent of teenagers!

Dr. James Dobson's book *Parenting Isn't for Cowards* expresses the reality of being a parent. It's *not* for cowards. Pain is always intertwined as a vital aspect in all our relationships, not only those with our children. Yet in the relationships with our children, we also have our hopes, aspirations, and ourselves all wrapped up in this investment. So as women we bear up under the pain of childbearing, while never begrudging the privilege of giving life.

In Adam's recognition of the life-giving capability of his wife, he names his bride Eve, the mother of all living. In this recognition and God's affirmation, all women share in both Eve's blessing and her penalty. We are Eve's daughters in being pain-bearers and life-givers.

The second result of the Fall was that the woman's relationship with and attitude toward her husband changed. They were co-rulers in paradise, equal by design in every way, with no relational conflict. Their recognizable differences, which were once delightful to the eye, now become an arena for conflict. In Larry Crabb's words, "Her personal attachment [to Adam] would involve heartache and battle."[10]

The Bible teaches that a wife is to be submissive to her husband (see Ephesians 5:22). *Subject (hupotasso)* is a military term meaning to place oneself under the authority of another.[11] This is a most unpopular concept in feminist circles today because it represents to them an inferior position. Perhaps this reaction has been caused in part by some Christian teaching that permitted, if not encouraged, men to dominate women in irrational and abusive ways.

However, in the same passage where women are told to submit, men are told to love their wives with the same unconditional love as Christ loves the Church. This depends on a great deal of mutual trust, sacrifice, and maturity from both the husband and wife in order to make the relationship work. Above all, it takes divine intervention and empowerment. (The passage begins in Ephesians 5:18 by asking both husbands and wives to be empowered by God's Spirit.) The Scriptures, it seems, view submission as the common lifestyle for all Christians, rather than the duty of women only. However, due to the Fall, women struggle with the reality of this judgment of submission.

God's judgment upon Adam differs from Eve's in that it relates not to his relationship with her, but to the relationship he maintains with his environment. Because Adam listened to the voice of his wife rather than to the command of God, the earth is cursed for his unique failure. Adam's relationship to his work would no longer be a joy and blessing. His work would take place in a difficult, hostile environment.

Women today are flocking to the workplace in order to find joy and meaning in their lives. But perhaps they should listen to the men who have been there. It is not the rewarding environment that women sometimes expect or want. In fact, it is more often than not a hostile, competitive, cut-throat world. Certainly their presence has brought needed feminine perspectives, but I doubt whether the workplace will really be transformed into caring communities simply because women are there! The thorns and thistles of the Fall are not gender-specific. Even the women who have done well and broken through the glass ceilings have often done it at the expense of most of their primary relationships.[12]

From the biblical perspective, work has not been designed to be a nurturing activity since sin entered the world. Many women have discovered that the world of work outside the home can be a harsh, destructive, and exhausting place. Men also have been used, abused, unappreciated, and victimized by their own hierarchical systems. Too many have sacrificed personal lives, families, and health to "scratch out a living." Is this what women want? Women, take heed!

## WOMEN OF MORTALITY

Before Adam and Eve were cast out of the garden, they were told that they would return to dust. The promise of physical immortality, as granted by the tree of life, was gone. What seemed to be a severe penalty may, in fact, have been a merciful act of God. Who would want to live forever in a fallen, aging state?

Death is now a reality. Mortality now stares all human beings in the face, whether we like it or not.

As a woman at the midpoint of life, I can attest to this downhill spiral. No matter how much money I spend on moisturizers and makeup, my skin will never return to the youthful elasticity I see on my daughters. I have heard that if you bend over and look into a mirror, your face will resemble how it will look at age sixty-five. I tried this one day when I was feeling particularly brave. What I saw was not a pretty sight! The downward pull of gravity was at work.

Not only has age taken its toll on my skin, but on my entire body. Everything is rearranged. I may weigh close to what I weighed twenty years ago, but it just doesn't look the same. When I look in the mirror I know this is as good as it's going to get. (I'll reserve my more extensive comments about the surgeon's knife for the next chapter.)

We women understand the frightful reality of mortality, but we fight it with every ounce of our strength, and a great deal of time and money. Our youth-crazed culture has thrown women into a mortal battle like never before. Plastic surgeons have never had it so good. Women can get a nip or a tuck, build up or suck out, and try to deny or postpone the aging process.

Due to medical advances, people do live longer. We want these additional years to be a time when we look and feel good. The pressure to be immortal confronts us every day on television, in magazines, and on the street. Now don't get me wrong. I'm all for feeling and looking good, but it requires more effort as time marches on. The feminist movement has focused on our brains and abilities, and has opened the doors of more working opportunities for all who choose to walk through. The advertizing industry has capitalized on this and teases us with promises of success and a sense of well-being as we walk through those doors using and wearing *their* products, of course.

The feminine journey has turned into a rat race as we try to keep up. As Bob writes in *The Masculine Journey*, "We may put it off for a while with cosmetics, exercise, and the surgeon's knife, but eventually the principle of the universe—decay—wins."[13] We are very mortal. As women we must realize and accept that our well-coiffed, manicured, firm, designer-clad, sweet-smelling body will one day end up in the bottom of a box, covered with dust.

This view of life is so far from most feminine minds, particularly youthful beauties. The young have an aura of invincibility surrounding them that endeavors to defy mortality. The young female who has just started her journey as a woman has yet to feel threatened by her inherent mortality, although it nips at her high heels from afar.

Her youthfulness is her power, her aura of enticement, her right. The young woman senses the power she wields, and sees it as her passage from childhood into adulthood. How little she understands beauty's potential for joy as well as its equal power to bring pain to herself and others.

This season of youthfulness is a powerful but fleeting period in a woman's life. Beauty is considered a excellent commodity in our society. It has become a false standard by which both men and women judge and evaluate other women. Therefore, this may be a painful rather than a positive time for a young woman. Some feel they have been cheated out of this commodity and lack power. Some feel that it has been the cause of their abuse and pain, considering their beauty something to be hidden or marred.

Inwardly, many women jealously yearn for the beautiful images they see on film, television, and in magazines. This "beauty myth" has become their god and the answer to all their problems. We must remember that as fallen and mortal women we can be easily deceived by the power of beauty.

This is a very important aspect of who we are and a necessary stop on the feminine journey. It is only one among many and passes quickly. A woman's journey necessitates that she root her identity in the creative handiwork of God, while also realizing her capability for deception and ultimate aging. For now, the next stop on this journey is to look at this mysterious alchemy of beauty . . . the young woman.

**"A Child"**
written by Candi Long

I remember very well when I was only eight,
I wanted to look all grown up standing by the gate;
And as the other children were naively walking by,
I wanted them to notice that I had passed them by.
I was older then . . . with high-heeled shoes, which were nice;
And the chairman of the P.T.A. often came to me for advice.

I was twelve one New Year's eve and waiting for my date,
Though he was imaginary, we stayed up awfully late;
We talked a lot about the war and bet on who would win
But when he tried to kiss my cheek, I said I had to go in.
I was older then . . . with a little rouge, which was nice;
And all my older sister's friends often came to me for advice.

Then when I was sixteen, I thought myself so cool;
I tried to join an older crowd and ended up the fool.
Amidst the drunken parties I sat very much alone,
But had entirely too much pride to ask to be taken home.
I was older then . . . with sophistication, which was nice;
And Abigail Van Buren often came to me for advice.

When I was in my 20's I gave my life to God;
But when I try to be His child, I find it awfully hard.
And yet He's taking all my years and letting people see
That He's making me the child of eight that I had forgotten how to be.
Hallelujah, I'm free.

CHAPTER THREE

# THE YOUNG WOMAN: THE ALCHEMY OF BEAUTY

❦

*Everything that deceives may be said to enchant.*
PLATO

*I cannot and will not cut my conscience
to fit this year's fashions.*
LILIAN HELLMAN

Last year I was given a six-month membership to a local health club. Although I had belonged to workout clubs in the past, since moving to Pennsylvania I had not participated in any serious exercise. Tennis, jogging, aerobic classes, and weight training were a part of my younger days. After the birth of each child I had faithfully worked out to try to regain my figure. My times at the health club were an opportunity to get away from the kids, associate with adults, and imagine that I was still that young, trim woman who could keep up no matter how tough the classes got. It became a personal challenge to do as many crunches as the younger girls in the class or even kick the highest during aerobics. As I reflect on those experiences, I think I was just desperately trying to convince myself that I was still young and attractive.

## THE OLDER WOMAN'S PERIL: AGING YOUTH

When I received a trial membership to a well-equipped health club, I was excited. I had been justifying my neglect of exercising by saying I needed the stimulating surroundings of a club complete with weight machines, instructors, and all the other amenities. However, once I had the membership, I found there was a tremendous hesitancy to use it. Joining a health club or gym can be one of the most threatening and demoralizing experiences a woman can have. Before, I felt confident exercising in the presence of other women and was energized by the experience. However, in my forties, it was different.

Time had marched on and so had my "youthful figure"! My workout clothes from the past, colored tights and leotards, were outdated. Now the accepted clothing of choice was the "thong" leotard over tight bicycle shorts or bubble-gum-pink spandex pants. "Step aerobics" had replaced the traditional aerobics class. This form of exercise involves complicated routines that leave you frustrated, convinced of your physical ineptitude, and totally exhausted. Bob's reaction to this insanity was, "I can't believe people pay to be humiliated like this!"

After a few sessions at the club, I found excuses not to go. I knew I needed the exercise, but it seemed so overwhelming; I felt left in the dust by these contemporary young women. They would race into the club on lunch breaks to perfect already incredible bodies that were taut, efficient engines of fitness, then shower and energetically race back to their jobs, beaming with the natural beauty of youth, of course. I left the club on the verge of cardiac arrest, sweating profusely, and just wanting to get home so I could lie down.

As I look back on my youth, I realize most young women never appreciate what they have until they've lost it. Let me make it very clear: I want to affirm these slim, fit and lovely girls in this stage of youthfulness. I only hope they choose to enjoy this time in their lives, and have a clear understanding of how to use their energy and beauty in positive ways. I hope they can feel good about themselves.

Unfortunately, many are unhappy and dissatisfied with what they see in the mirror. Youth has a tendency to focus on the blemishes, flaws, scars, birthmarks, and differences, viewing them as imperfections rather than those elements that make each of us a unique expression of God's creativity. I have found that with age comes a larger perspective that allows me to view myself in an entirely more accepting rather than condemning way.

As far as physical appearance and conditioning go, when most of us look into the mirror we have to say, "This may be as good as it's going to get." The older the body gets, the more maintenance it requires. Motherhood and babies push and stretch the stomach outward, and eventually gravity begins its downward pull as the beauty of youth begins to fade.

However, women are proving they are more than artifacts of

beauty and ornaments to grace the arms of men. Women today have unparalleled opportunities due to the radical activities of the sixties and the rebirth of feminism in the seventies. Women can now obtain the highest educational levels and even do such things as fly combat jets. They have entered into the professional and work arenas once dominated by men, and have claimed legal rights to their bodies and reproductive abilities. Many have seriously challenged the traditional beliefs about their feminine gender roles.

Women have never enjoyed more opportunities for freedom. Yet they do not seem to be experiencing the inner peace and contentment they expected would accompany this liberation. Best-selling author and researcher Naomi Wolf comments in her book, *Beauty Myth*, "Recent research consistently shows that inside the majority of the West's controlled, attractive, successful working women, there is a secret 'underlife' poisoning our freedom; infused with notions of beauty, it is a dark vein of self-hatred, physical obsessions, terror of aging and dread of lost control."[1]

## THE YOUNG WOMAN'S TERROR: LOW SELF-ESTEEM

As I look back upon my past feelings about my self-image and my body, I remember the deep insecurities and fears I had. My twin and I are fraternal, and have always been very different in size and appearance. My sister, Cathy, was much smaller than I was and still remains so. I was not a heavy child until about the fourth grade, when I experienced a growth spurt in height and weight. My athletic tendencies began to manifest themselves.

In the fifth grade, a very routine event at school brought to the surface the beginning of my acute awareness of "fear of fat." The school nurse was routinely weighing all the children in our school. She came to our room and lined everyone up, marching us single file down to her office. She proceeded to weigh us one by one. To my shock and horror, I was the only girl in my class to weigh over 100 pounds (103 pounds to be exact). Isn't it funny how that number has stuck in my mind all these years! I felt embarrassed and ashamed. To make matters worse, I also wore glasses and had braces. I thought I was a mess!I was also the only girl in the class to need a bra. My mother continually had to remind me to wear one because I would conveniently forget. Of course, Cathy got one too, but it was a "training" bra. (That term has always intrigued me. What is the bra training?)

Due to my athletic bent, through junior and senior high school I was involved in competitive swimming and diving, and became quite an accomplished water skier. While most of my friends would sit on the boat dock in their two-piece bathing suits, I was skiing with the boys in my sturdy one-piece. I was always trying to outdo them. I was also proud of the fact that I could slalom better than any other girl around.

One day while I was combing my hair, one of my friends looked at my arms and remarked, "You look like an Amazon woman with those arms." I instantly lowered my arms, became very self-conscience, and seldom wore sleeveless blouses from that point on. However, today I'm proud of the physical strength and muscle tone of my upper arms. I won't have the flabby arms that so many older women have.

My "fat" mentality has continued to plague me through the years. It has also put a great deal of pressure on my two daughters and has caused them unnecessary pain as I projected this image on them. Particularly as a result of being raised in the South, I may be too concerned about how I look. Because a woman's appearance has so much riding on it (like one's entire self-esteem), her looks become overly important.

One night while I was watching television, a disturbing but enlightening program was aired. The title was "The Famine Within." This documentary explored the problem of young women in North America starving themselves to death through anorexia (not eating) or bulimia (the bingeing and purging of food). This disorder is an epidemic among females, striking over a million American women every year. Young women, at alarming rates, are on self-inflicted starvation programs. For some these disorders stem from an obsessive fixation on food denial as a means to achieve the beauty image portrayed by the media as perfection. Many of the models and Hollywood personalities who have become the hallmark for the "perfect" woman admit to suffering from eating disorders. Thin is in!

Experts agree that 5 to 10 percent of all American girls and women are anorectic. The film I viewed cites a study done in San Francisco of 494 middle-class, elementary school girls. Over 80 percent of the fourth grade girls were on a diet. However, only about 15 percent of the girls studied were actually overweight. One little girl interviewed said she would rather be dead than fat.

This obsession with thinness violates the uniqueness of a woman's body and prohibits its true expression. Fat is vitally important to the female body. Women have on average 8 percent more body fat as compared to men for a reason.[2] The fat tissues regulate the hormone balance necessary for reproduction, good health, and sexual desire. Excessive exercise, over-dieting, and loss of fat deny women their femininity and result in an asexual being.

Americans sit in front of our television sets night after night, watching in horror and shock as the starving faces of those in Third World and war-torn countries invade the comfort and security of our homes. We struggle with frustration over the powerlessness we feel, as individuals or as a country, to alleviate these atrocities. Yet we tragically ignore the self-inflicted hunger of our own daughters in affluent North America.

They starve themselves daily in order to conform to the insane social reality that the beautiful woman is the thin woman. According to Dr. Michael Strober in an article in *People* magazine, "A woman becomes anorexic because her soul has been battered by the unreasonable expectation that you can never be too thin and that fat—any fat—equals failure."[3] This is a disorder of middle and upper class women, not the poor. In an ironic twist, the poor can't eat, and the rich won't eat.

The women's movement sought the answer to the low self-esteem problem by freeing women from the bondage of domesticity and thrusting them into the "freedom" of the 9 to 5 work regimen. Little did they realize that young women would create their own self-imposed prisons, denying the body's need for food.

Naomi Wolf, in *The Beauty Myth*, theorizes that new chains of the "perfect body" and the "super woman" have replaced the chains of domestic bondage. Somehow the super woman became the image and goal for women in the nineties. Her image included, all at once, the roles of Donna Reed as the professional housewife, Murphy Brown as the professional career woman, and Jane Fonda as the professional beauty. What a lineup! And what a tough act to follow!

Recently a new look for women has been introduced by top fashion designers on the leading runways of Europe. The super-models are described by the *Dallas Morning News* as "the glamour Amazons with their hyper hair, teeth and curves are being edged out by a budding crop of 'gamines' [street urchins]. They are wan, wistful, doe-eyed and as thin as adolescent boys."[4] The article cites several possible reasons for this new image. Some feel it is a reaction to the oversaturation of the super-models. They suggest the idea of a fashion pendulum that is constantly swinging back and forth, from one extreme to another, as the explanation. Another idea is that fashion does not have a pendulum effect but is merely a mirror reflecting the feelings and expressions of the time. One sociologist thinks that the "waif" image and the "grunge" look reflect a period of economic ditress and poverty. She writes that "we feel vulnerable and the 'waif' reflects that image."[5]

Feminist writers such as Naomi Wolf in *The Beauty Myth* and Susan Faludi in *Backlash* hold to a conspiratorial explanation for the beauty images and their resultant messages. Faludi writes, "The stronger and more grownup women become in real life, the greater the tendency to portray women as helpless and little-girl-like in the fantasy world of fashion and beauty."[6]

Finally, a more positive belief held by some is that this "anti-fashion" rise of the "gamine" image is a rebellious declaration that "beauty comes in many forms."[7] I wish that were true. Unfortunately for the millions of women in North America, whatever reigns as the current image of beauty is seldom attainable. The result is a rampant epidemic of low self-esteem. Women seem prone to falling into one deceptive trap after another in search of the perfect image of self. We seem trapped by a cult of perfection. The beauty myth that projects the *Vogue* image of the gaunt, anorectic, youthful model or the "power body" of the muscularly defined, well-chiseled frame have replaced the "power suit" and supplanted the happy housewife as the arbiter of successful womanhood.

When all is said and done, the voice of society has not changed in almost 150 years. That voice still echoes the sentiments of 1852 as recorded in *Godey's Lady's Book*, the fashion magazine of its day: "It is the woman's business to be beautiful."[8] Common aphorisms such as "'Woman' embodies the ideal of beauty" and "Beauty is particularly a female perfection" still plague women today.[9]

Having raised two daughters through the trauma of the teenage years, I am keenly aware of the distress young women face as they struggle with the concept of beauty. From my middle-aged perspective, when I look at our girls I see beautiful, naturally glowing skin without wrinkles. Their bodies are tight, firm, and free from cellulite. Their persona has a vitality and vulnerability of spirit that has yet to be exhausted and daunted by the demands and disappointments of life.

As I look in the mirror today, I know if I had the young face and energetic body of my youth, I would appreciate it and be satisfied. Now all I can do is watch home movies taken when I was sixteen, water skiing on the lake and going to the senior prom, and take it by faith that I was young once. My mother told me, as she took these movies so many years ago, "You'll love looking at these when you're pregnant or when your children are this age, and you can remember how wonderful it was to be young."

Unfortunately, youth is such a painful stage on a woman's journey. One might refer to it as "the best of times and the worst of times." Young girls have a distorted image of themselves as they look through the lens of the super-models and Hollywood starlets. My daughters subscribe to beauty and fashion magazines for young women. I recently read through several issues of Ashley's *Allure* magazine in preparation for this chapter. Even the title of the magazine illustrates the philosophy that lies behind the pages of beauty tips, glamour, and advice on women's issues. The word *allure* means, "to tempt with something desirable; attract, entice."[10]

Within the pages of this magazine and others like it, young women are lured by the hidden messages of the images of beauty and by the promises and hopes that if you use the products advertised within, you too can achieve perfection. One article was entitled, "Trapped by Perfection: In a world where media images are frighteningly perfect, what's an ordinary person to do?" The writer says,

> When you look at a supermodel perpetually frozen in elegance and unresolved suggestion, you look at a world in which life is arrested in a flat tableau of uncomplicated personas. In this world there is no room for uneven fingernails, crow's-feet, flawed teeth, farting, or letting your stomach hang out. Heck, there's no room to have a bad cold. There is certainly no room for ungainly, often unbeautiful emotion. There is no room for you.[11]

What is even more tragic is that the images portrayed by the models in magazines are illusions. Naomi Wolf writes, "Fashion magazine editors acknowledged at last the existence of the Scitex machine—a computer graphics machine that alters almost every fashion or glamour image we see. Research has found that young women's self-esteem scored measurably lower after they were shown fashion and beauty images than before."[12]

How did women get sucked into this beauty myth? What are the historical roots that created these images of beauty? Each era seems to have its own perception of the perfect woman, proceeds to deify it, and then beckons all women to bow at the feet of the idol, ascribing worship and granting bondage to its every demand. For a young woman to enjoy this stage of her journey, she must recognize and come to terms with the power this beauty image has on her life. She must begin to see beauty in more critical terms. A good way to begin is by looking at the wisdom provided in the Holy Scriptures.

## BEAUTY: THE POWER OF THE YOUNG WOMAN

Scripture confirms that on a woman's journey the season of youthfulness is a normal stage. It is a time of magnetic-magical attraction to the opposite sex, a time when one's appearance gains and grants tremendous power.

The New Testament word for young woman—*parthenos*—picks up many of the meanings and usages found in the Hebrew Old Testament (*bethulah* and *'almah*). From the New Testament perspective, the emphasis on the young woman is her unmarried state and her sexual purity. Often, as in the case of Mary, the mother of Jesus, her virginity is a major issue in the development of God's miraculous involvement. (See Isaiah 7:14 in relation to Matthew 1:23.) Therefore, the idea of the young woman includes the related ideas of sexual power because of her purity or virginity. One linguist noted, "The emphasis lies less upon chastity than upon youthful vitality with its magical power."[13]

When the Old Testament is consulted, the major theme of the young woman centers around her aspect of beauty. Beauty is not gender specific; Joseph, David, and Absalom are all called handsome or beautiful by the biblical writers (see Genesis 39:6, 1 Samuel 16:12, and 2 Samuel 14:25). However, the main use of the Hebrew word for "beauty"—*yapheh*—relates to the young woman and feminine imagery. The conclusion is not difficult: In biblical usage, the power of the young woman lies in her beauty.

Biblical writers often allude to this power of youthful beauty women have to influence events, decisions, and actions, for good or ill. Sarah is a beautiful young woman, so beautiful her husband feels he must lie to protect her (see Genesis 12:11-13). Rachel "got her man" by being beautiful in both form (body) and countenance (face) (see Genesis 29:17). Abigail, one of David's wives, is called beautiful in both appearance and intelligence (see 1 Samuel 25:3). David's nurse and final companion was Abisag, called *very* beautiful (see

1 Kings 1:3-4). Queen Esther won the Persian national beauty pageant by being beautiful in form and face (see Esther 2:7). God rewards Job with daughters so beautiful that no one in the land can be compared to them (see Job 42:15).

The advantage (or liability) for the beautiful young women is also seen in the guidance given for Israel's warfare. When their army obtained victories over enemies, and the soldiers were attracted to the beauty of the captured women, they could take these women for themselves, but only after the women were allowed a time of mourning for their parents (presumed killed in battle). Then the women could be taken into the men's households only if they were properly regarded as wives (see Deuteronomy 21:11). Depending upon one's perspective, these attractive women either found security and legal status as benefits of their beauty or were ripped away from their homeland against their will because of their beauty.

Tamar, the beautiful daughter of King David, is an example of how beauty became her greatest liability. Her half-brother Amnon became obsessed with her beauty and raped her (2 Samuel 13:1-19). The consequences of this sexual abuse affected many people. Throughout history, a woman's beauty has continued to make her vulnerable to the desires of men and their destructive behavior.

Once a woman has been sexually abused she considers her beauty as a risk, something to be feared, protected against, and even destroyed. Young women go to various extremes to render themselves unattractive and "safe" from further abuse. These extremes include extreme weight loss or gain, as well as inflicting personal physical injury in an attempt to disfigure themselves. Beauty and femininity for a sexually abused woman becomes a curse and may cause her to inflict whatever damage to herself is necessary to avoid a relationship with a man and the risk of being hurt again. If you identify with this problem, the chapter on the wounded woman deals with sexual abuse in more detail.

The wisdom literature of the Old Testament views the beautiful woman in both positive and negative ways: She is the personification of wisdom (see Proverbs 1:20); the sensually beautiful, love-making wife (see Song of Solomon); and the alluring, adulterous woman (see Proverbs 5:3-14). When the prophets use the imagery of a beautiful woman, it is often associated with the pagan idols God's people made in lieu of worshiping the true God. They would "beautify" wood and stone images with gold and silver in order to create "feminine" idols (see Jeremiah 10:1-4). The prophet Jeremiah chides Israel, saying, "What are you doing, O devastated one? Why dress yourself in scarlet and put on jewels of gold? Why shade your eyes with paint? You adorn yourselves in vain" (Jeremiah 4:30, NIV).

Throughout Israel's history a cultural and religious tension existed with her pagan neighbors. They worshiped false gods and erected elaborate images to their tribute. These, of course, were always fashioned and carved by human hands, which was in direct violation of the First and Second Commandments given by God to Moses (see Exodus 20:3-4). For the Israelites, giving visual imagery of any kind to the invisible God was tantamount to spiritual adultery. God considered the nation to be a spiritually undefiled virgin, a young maiden of divine beauty. But she become adulterous when she played around with the gods of the other nations (see Jeremiah 18:13, Hosea 13:2).

What is interesting is how deeply interrelated the concepts of sexuality and spirituality are to an understanding of God's relationship to Israel in using this feminine metaphor of the nation. In fact, through all of ancient history, sexuality and spirituality are united. It is only in the late Greek philosophical period that a certain dualism sets in whereby sexuality and issues of worship become separated.

To this day, sexuality is not a subject to be openly discussed in the church because we must deal with "spiritual" issues there. At the same time, issues of sexuality have become the open domain of psychologists, talk-show hosts, and the entire media industry. Individuals who would never mention that they have anything to do with "spiritual things" (except maybe some New Age, feel-good philosophy) will talk about sex all day long.

Perhaps to better understand what is happening in regard to the worship of beauty among women and men, we must look back. Then we can see that early in the history of religion sexuality based on beauty was very much a spiritual subject, and not set apart as it is in this modern secular period. Indeed, one writer notes that to combine these two elements "presents a paradox to our logical minds; we are disinclined to associate that which is sexual with that which is consecrated to the gods."[14]

In Bob's book, *The Masculine Journey*, he discusses the phallic stage of a man's life and comments about seeing some Hawaiian artifacts (wood idols) where the image's penis was quite large and erect. He said at that time his response was, "Things never really change."

He was alluding to the fact that the enlarged phallic symbol so common in both gay and straight pornography has some ancient kinship. Our phallus-focused society today is no different from ancient ones.

The same is true for women today. The feminine ideal of beauty has always been a significant aspect of ritual worship. In a serious study of the "sacred prostitute," author Nancy Qualls-Corbett writes about this goddess of passion:

> The goddess of love, passion and fertility was known by various names at different times and in different places. . . . In Greece, she was the beautiful Aphrodite. Aphrodite was not associated with fertility—Aphrodite reigned over love and passion, and her image is perhaps the most renowned for these attributes today. Regardless of her name or locale, the goddess of love is associated with springtime, with nature in bloom, the time when seeds burst forth in splendor. *Beauty* [emphasis mine] is the quintessential component; Aphrodite's nakedness is glorified. She is the only goddess to be portrayed nude in classical sculptures. The loveliness of her feminine body is adored and adorned.[15]

Right now, as I leaf through a book revealing actual photographs of some of these images, I am amazed. Clay goddesses from Cyprus show enlarged hips emphasizing the feminine vulva. Their arms are wrapped around breasts with well-defined nipples. Pictures of stone sculptured goddesses, from the pre-Mycenaean era of Crete, are just as striking. They are mostly faceless, with the only clear details being breasts and vaginal area. A picture of Ishtar, the goddess of love, reveals a head full of long, flowing hair and enlarged breasts. A faceless moon goddess from Egypt has arms outstretched toward the sky (moon) with two breasts as the only detail on a nondescript body. Aphrodite, of course, is made to be the perfection of both the human and divine body. Though headless and armless (not by design), it is a perfectly formed body by even modern standards. The hourglass shape includes rounded breasts complete with nipples and extreme detail in the pelvic area.

We can look at pictures of these goddesses in books and actually view them in the great museums of the world. But when we do, most people merely admire them as "nice" works of art. We praise the sculptors or get involved in detailed discussions as to what period they date from. Usually we miss the important point, or fail to ask the critical questions about these "beauties"—the question "Why?" What purpose did these ideal images of beauty serve in the ancient world? It is very easy to write them off as "pagan pornography" or "Egyptian artwork from the late bronze age," and forget they played a very important function in daily life and how the common people expressed their worship.

These carved statues functioned very much like *Vogue* models and *Playboy* centerfolds of today. They were the ideal feminine forms to be pursued, cultivated, and worshiped. They were the representations of the gods and goddesses. They found their real-life counterparts in the ancient temples where, as sacred prostitutes, young beautiful women became mediatrixes between the gods and humans.

Imagine for a moment the Greek Parthenon (Greek for "virginal young woman"), one of the Seven Wonders of the World. What happened there? This was where priestesses, the goddesses of love, were concealed behind candle-lit veils, creating an aura of mystery. Sacred young women of perfect proportions would then take strangers into their inner love sanctuaries and kneel before the image of Venus or another goddess of passion and love. The woman would pray that their "offering of love" would be received. Both individuals believed (if they were orthodox!) that in the consummation of their love-act, a magical transformation would take place.

The maiden was initiated into the fullness of womanhood. The male stranger, likewise, was changed forever. Qualls-Corbett notes,

> The qualities of the receptive feminine nature, so opposite from
> his own, are embedded deep within his soul; the image of the
> sacred prostitute is viable within him. He is fully aware of the
> deep emotions within the sanctuary of his heart. He makes no spe-
> cific claims on the woman herself, but carries her image, the per-
> sonification of love and sexual joy, into the world. His experience
> of the mysteries of sex and religion opens the door to the potential
> of on-going life; it accompanies the regeneration of the soul.[16]

This is powerful stuff! Having made love to this perfection of beauty, the male then carries her image in his soul for the rest of his life and receives regenerative strength from the experience. This is very much how the images of perfect women are carried every day in the minds of both sexes.

For women, it might be a picture of a gorgeous model gracing the cover of *Cosmopolitan*. At one time or another each one us may have placed a picture on our bathroom mirror or refrigerator representing how we want to look. This image motivates us through our diets or exercise routines until we make this image ours. The picture is the motivation and source of strength not to eat or to go jogging.

For men, it is the air-brushed centerfold of perfection that adorns their locker, dorm room, or work site. Likewise, she is the image in men's head of what a woman should look like. Having encountered the goddess and worshiped her, they now carry her ideal in their heads throughout life.

Bob has often taught that at the core of most addictions—whether sexual, chemical, or relational—lies idolatry.[17] Worshiping a false god, though perfect and experientially exciting, can be very addictive. Having tasted of the drug, many are hooked for life. We can all get hooked on what makes us feel good. Until we understand that addictions, compulsions, and obsessions—whether they be sexual, chemical, or relational—are very much rooted in pleasurable experiences, we haven't really embraced the power of deception that is at work in our lives.

Solomon was wise in encouraging his sons to stay clear of the Parthenon and other houses where the beautiful woman and her pleasure couch awaited her prey (see Proverbs 5:7-11). Solomon must have known that once he experienced such a place, the young man was hooked for life to his own destruction.

The worship of beauty in young "perfect" women is what drives and energizes much of this fallen world. It is far more than commercial and financial. I don't think it can be explained or explained away on such simplistic terms. At its core lies an amalgam of personal identity issues, sexual desire, and spiritual power. We will all worship divinity with our bodies because they were made to be the physical agents of our spiritual commitments. Our bodies are essentially spiritual as well as material. But within this creational attribute lies the fallen, dark-sided reality that through the worship of beauty our bodies can become agents of pagan gods.

It took the modern world to absolutely commercialize and market the power of the young woman.

## THE AMERICAN PURSUIT OF BEAUTY

In a monumental study of the social history of women, writer Lois Banner explains,

The pursuit of personal beauty has always been a central concern of American women. The pursuit of beauty and of its attendant features, fashion and dress has more than any other factor bound together women of different classes, regions, and ethnic groups and constituted a key element in women's separate experience of life.[18]

Banner points out one central theme in the literature about women in the nineteenth century: "That beauty for women represented not morality but power. 'From the memorable day when the queen of Sheba made a formal call on the lamented King Solomon, the power of beauty has controlled the fate of dynasties and the lives of men.'"[19]

In Banner's opinion, the ideal woman's characteristics have differed throughout history, but in the nineteenth century the one common denominator that began to transcend time and place was the image of the young woman. Banner writes, "The central characteristic . . . and one that contrasted with previous beauty models—was that she was young. Her youth underscored her purity and reflected both the nineteenth-century romanticization of childhood and its tendency to infantize women, to view them as creatures of childlike dispositions."[20]

The disadvantage of this American pursuit of beauty lies in the fact women have fallen prey to the very unattractive qualities of narcissism and consumerism.

By the late nineteenth century an elaborate system of symbols, rules, and rewards had arisen to reinforce the Cinderella mythology. Popular working-class novels focused on marriages between working women and wealthy men. Newspapers and magazines featured the lives of actresses—increasingly powerful style setters—who had often risen to prominence from humble backgrounds. By 1900 the chorus girl had become a major exemplar of beauty's success, for she was generally of working-class background and, after her day of glamour, usually married a millionaire, according to popular belief. At the same time, the commercial beauty culture provided increasingly complex makeup, coiffures, and clothes by means of which the ordinary woman could copy the heroine of the hour. Finally, in the early nineteenth century the category of "beauty" or "belle" developed among both working and wealthy women to denominate style setters in the area of physical appearance. In the wake of this development, hundreds of beauty contests occurred to ritualize beauty competition among women.

The decades from the 1920s to the 1980s involved the further development of trends and institutions already established before World War I. Of all the years of this century, 1921 was a pivotal date in the history of women's looks. Not only did a major shift in beauty standards occur about that time, but that year also marked the start of Atlantic City's Miss America Pageant, the most famous and longest-running of all American beauty contests. The event made a national ritual of the by then powerful notion that the pursuit of beauty ought to be a woman's primary goal.[21]

The beautiful woman has now become our queen, complete with diamond-studded, regal crowns, surrounded by smiling but jealous attendants (losers), and standing before her devoted and adoring subjects. We have all crowned her Miss America and made her the ideal beauty for all women. Every year millions of little girls sit glued to their television set watching the Miss America Pageant. They fantasize that one day they, too, will take that long walk down the runway wearing that glittering crown. This pageant may represent the hopes and dreams of many little girls, but at a tremendous cost to the average woman's self-esteem and happiness.

So where has all this pursuit and worship of beauty led us? Right back to that exercise club I joined but never really used! Why didn't I use it? Because my ideal of the perfect woman had become a god. The youthful appearance, the unlined face, hair without any sign of gray, a slim body with good muscle tone had become my goddess.

I had worshiped at the altar of a god with a very long pedigree: Isis, Ishtar, Venus, Aphrodite, the Medieval virgins, the frail Victorian maidens, the Flapper era's Clara Bow, the erotic silent film vamps portrayed by Theda Bara and Greta Garbo, the young Katharine Hepburn, Bette Davis, Claudette Colbert, and Marlene Dietrich. Then came the "mammary goddesses" with their childlike voluptuousness: Ava Gardner, Jane Russell, Jane Mansfield, and of course, Marilyn Monroe.[22] Throw in Brigitte Bardot, Cheryl Tiegs, Christie Brinkley, Cindy Crawford, Sharon Stone, and Madonna, and you can see why I felt so inadequate simply to work up a sweat!

It seems clear that from the biblical culture continuing for centuries to contemporary society, the power of the young woman is her beauty. It can be a thing of great value, of time-consuming vanity, or of damaging pain.

Now the question remains: If this aspect of a woman's life is so dominant, how can we as women put it in a better perspective? What is it we need to teach the young women in our society about this phase (and it is just a phase) of the journey? What do I need to tell my daughters? What should I have already taught them about this so important season of life? What do I wish my mother had taught me?

Again, I believe the ancient wisdom from the Scriptures brings a balanced perspective for the young woman. I believe we can draw four conclusions about the biblical young woman and her relation to beauty.

## Beauty Is an Issue of the Spirit

The old cliché "Beauty is only skin deep" is not quite accurate. Hopefully, by looking at the ancient and contemporary mythologies surrounding the beauty theme, one can see that much more is going on here. This power of beauty is something that is very mysterious, lying deep within the recesses of the human spirit. The power is much more than merely trying to look good! No, the issues are much deeper; they are issues of the heart and spirit, something that can be explained only by looking deep within the structure of human sexuality itself.

Why is this so? Returning to chapter 1, we saw how the Creator fashioned a unique feminine being as a companion for the male, Adam: "And God created them, male and female" (Genesis 1:27). The Hebrew word *neqevah*, used to express the English word *female*, has as its root the meaning of "to pierce, or bore through something."[23] It carries the idea of something having had a hole pierced through it. Several nouns are also formed from this word, nouns that are translated as "hole" or "cavity" or "tunnel."[24]

The anatomical implications here are quite obvious. Being female means being defined by our unique vaginal opening. Our male counterparts are also defined by their anatomy in the Hebrew word for male (*zakar*). Both sexes have been given very sophisticated and delicate sexual organs by the Creator, which are made to fit together.[25]

Herein lies the raw, inherent spiritual power that causes men and women to be attracted to each other, and to go to extremes to obtain each other's attention. The mysterious, often irrational compulsion two individuals have for one another who are so unlike each other is explainable only from the spiritual reality of creation. The currency most women use in order to bring this attraction about is the currency of beauty.

Here the beautiful woman portrait carried by a man must coincide with the reality he sees in a woman. If she fits the fantasy of his "dream woman," a relationship can happen. Likewise, if he fits her fantasy (usually the Prince Charming theme), the magical quality is present. A spell is woven and for a moment in time, everything else in the world ceases to exist.

This magical quality that both are looking for is a deeply spiritual thing. It transcends mere biological chemistry. Animals go through their mating routines apparently without all this mythology and fantasy. Most join, mate, and then leave. Very uncomplicated. But for the young woman, her view of beauty and appearance will always be making a statement about the god she serves and whatever spiritual commitments she maintains.

In the final analysis, what the young woman needs to learn during this season of life is where to place her trust, along with a healthy knowledge of what she should fear. As women, we are raised to fear being fat more than to have a fear of God. Some of us wouldn't think of getting caught without our makeup on. Is this because we fear the rejection of those who "might" see us more than being concerned about pleasing our Creator?

In an extended allegory, the prophet Ezekiel laments the mistaken notion that the nation of Israel held in trusting in her beauty. He writes,

> You [Jerusalem] were adorned with gold and silver; your clothes were of fine linen, costly fabric and embroidered cloth. Your food was fine flour, honey and olive oil. You become very beautiful and rose to be a queen. And your fame spread among the nations on account of your beauty, because the splendor I had given you made your beauty perfect, declares the Sovereign LORD. But you trusted in your beauty and used your fame to become a prostitute. You lavished your favors on anyone who passed by and your beauty became his. You took some of your garments to make gaudy high places, where you carried on your prostitution. (Ezekiel 16:13-16, NIV)

A young woman's beauty is a spiritual issue because it reveals that in which she trusts. I can place my faith and trust in my good looks (or in my mind, my career, or my husband's career), or I can honor God with whatever and however I look. In all things, whether beautiful or not, I need to seek to please Him. In doing so, I am learning to trust in God rather than in the beauty myth.

But if the power of the young woman is essentially tied to spiritual things, then it must also be recognized that the deceptive forces at work in a woman's life are also spirit-based.

## Beauty Is Deceptive

In doing the research for this book, I kept asking myself why it seems women have been so duped by the promises of diets, makeup, and advertising. Today women are not satisfied with covering up flaws with makeup or hair color, but have resorted to much more drastic measures. The cosmetic surgery industry thrives thanks to the warped female perception of beauty, grossing over $300 million per year with annual increases of 10 percent.[26] Women are willing to subject themselves to dangerous implants that have proven to leak into the body, undeniably causing illness and death. The chemical peeling of skin is comparable to second degree burns. Add to this the effects of repeated cosmetic facial surgery that leaves women looking inhuman or like clones.

Naomi Wolf is very blunt: "Cosmetic surgery is not 'cosmetic' and human flesh is not 'plastic.' Even the names trivialize what it is. It's not like ironing wrinkles in fabric, or tuning up a car, or altering outmoded clothes. Trivialization and infantilization pervade the surgeons' language they use when they speak to women: a 'nip,' a 'tummy tuck.'"[27]

I don't mean to imply that all cosmetic surgery is wrong. Plastic surgery is a blessing to those who have been disfigured through accidents or illnesses. However, I know lovely sixteen-year-old girls who have already had plastic surgery to change their noses or liposuction to remove extra fat. What a sad commentary when the beauty of youth goes under the surgeon's knife even before it has had an opportunity to mature. Dr. Robert Goldwyn, in his book *The Patient and the Plastic Surgeon*, comments on the current obsession of "plastisurgiholics": "[It] constitutes a syndrome of our era: the compulsive pursuit of perfection in the hope for happiness, the latter becoming more elusive as the chase becomes fiercer."[28]

Some blame a masculine conspiracy that keeps women poor, insecure, dependent, and dissatisfied. Women remain in bondage to this beauty myth thus maintaining financial profit and control by men. This may potentially be true.

But again I think this explanation does not go deep enough. The power at work in women is from far more than either an economic or gender conspiracy. Behind all the beauty creams, diets, exercise routines, and cosmetic surgery stands the deceiver we first met in the garden. His scheme from day one has been to put before women's eyes (and men's) a false image of the beautiful, while making the promise that in pursuing this image she would be more fulfilled and happy: "When the woman saw that the fruit of the tree was good for food and pleasing to the eye, and also desirable for gaining wisdom, she took and ate" (Genesis 3:6, NIV). She swallowed the lie!

What we find in this shrewd, cunning serpent is both the personification of deceptive evil and the perfection of beauty. The prophet Ezekiel laments over this fallen prince of creation, who was called king of Tyre (one who rules over the rulers of human cities):

> The word of the LORD came to me: "Son of man, take up a lament concerning the king of Tyre and say to him: 'This is what the Sovereign LORD says:
>
> "'You were the model of perfection,
>     full of wisdom and perfect in beauty.
> You were in Eden,
>     the garden of God;
> every precious stone adorned you:
>     ruby, topaz, and emerald,
>     chrysolite, onyx and jasper,
>     sapphire, turquoise and beryl.
> Your settings and mountings were made of gold;
>     on the day you were created they were prepared.
> You were anointed as a guardian cherub,
>     for so I ordained you. . . .
> So I drove you in disgrace from the mount of God
>     and I expelled you, O guardian cherub,
>     from among the fiery stones.
> Your heart became proud
>     on account of your beauty,
> and you corrupted your wisdom
>     because of your splendor.
> So I threw you to the earth.'" (Ezekiel 28:11-14,16-17; NIV)

"Diamonds," as the old song says, "are a girl's best friend!" Actually, these "friends" were designer originals for someone other than women. The precious stones of this earth that we are so enamored with were created to adorn Satan before he was cast out of God's presence. Satan knows a great deal about beauty and its power because he was and probably still is the most perfect specimen of beauty.

At creation, this serpentine deceiver was no medieval devil, complete with horns and forked tail. When God created the angelic hosts, He pulled out all the stops when it came to His chief guardian cherub. All the material wealth of this world—gold, silver, diamonds, and other precious stones—were created for him. But rather than valuing this beauty as a gift of God's goodness, he became so proud that he wanted no other rivals, even God.[29]

Is it any wonder, then, that behind much of the beauty industry, even the compulsions and addictions related to beauty, lies this ancient foe. The New Testament clearly reveals Satan's character and strategy. He is a deceiver, approaching us as an angel of light (and beauty) (see 2 Corinthians 11:14). His strategic plan for gaining our attention is through lies. Jesus Himself said, "He is a liar and the father of all lies" (John 8:44).

So pervasive is Satan's corrupted nature that there is absolutely no truthfulness in his being. We can't even imagine such a being. We have all had experiences with people who regularly tell lies, but try to imagine what it would be like not even to possess the capability for telling the truth!

This creature is also a murderer and destroyer who desires to steal from us our allegiance to God, and the creational self-esteem that God has provided both in creation and in Christ (John 8:44, 10:10). This means that women have a very formidable foe working overtime behind the scenes. Behind much of this pursuit of beauty, which only robs women of their self-estimate and contentment with who they are, is *the* person of beauty, Lucifer himself, the shining morning star. He works overtime on our minds, getting us to believe a host of lies about ourselves, our lives, and our looks! Then, his deception of us in turn creates further deceptive relationships with ourselves, our female friends, even with our God.

We think we are "okay" because we look good, or we think we are "not okay" because we don't look good. Either way, we have believed a lie, a lie given birth by a centuries-old deceiver who does not want us to believe that we are acceptable simply because we are in Christ. It is God—no one else!—who justifies me and makes me acceptable before Him, no matter how I look before other women, my husband, or the world (see Romans 3:22-26).

Do we then conclude this discussion of the young woman's beauty by talking about the chief antagonist of the universe, Lucifer? No. Though Satan was God's purist expression of beauty in the original creation, beauty does not begin with the serpent.

### Beauty Is a Divine Attribute

Ultimately, beauty begins with God. He created the world with color, taste, fragrance, feel, and sound. He created human beings in His own image, with the capability of making distinctions of taste, sight, smell, texture, and noise. With each of these senses comes an entire range of possibility of what we as humans might deem as beautiful. In one century, plump women were beautiful, while the skinny ones were ugly, only to have a complete reversal of taste in another century. The concept of beauty and what is considered beautiful by any given culture or group will always change.

But beauty is not only in the eye of the beholder; it is also in the eye of our Maker. The psalmist attributes beauty to Zion, the city of our God, saying, "Out of Zion, the perfection of beauty, God has shone forth" (Psalm 50:2). "Beautiful in elevation, the joy of the whole earth, is Mount Zion in the far north, the city of the great King" (48:2). Zion, of course, is both the literal city of Jerusalem, where God's name should be honored around the world, and the symbol of the presence of God among His people.

In other words, the place where God dwells is infused with a certain sense of beauty. There is something very pleasing about the presence of God among His people. This was probably the thought in David's mind when he wrote "Behold, how good and pleasant [beautiful] it is for brethren to dwell together in unity" (Psalm 133:1, KJV). After this statement, he picks up the element of the senses. He says this beautiful unity is both sweet smelling (precious oil upon the head) and refreshing (like the dew of Hermon).

I am not a student of ancient cities, but I would imagine that there were many cities in the ancient world more beautiful than Jerusalem. What made Zion unique, special, and beautiful was the fact that God had chosen that place to make His name manifested among His people. When one went up to Zion to worship, something very beautiful was taking place. This was a beauty not linked to personal appearance, but to the worship of the true and living God.

The same is true today. We as women must learn to find more of our beauty in the corporate experience of meeting and worshiping God.

Maybe this is what the apostles Paul and Peter were trying to encourage in the first-century women. Instead of focusing their lives on shopping for and wearing costly garments (see 1 Timothy 2:9), they should develop the inner qualities of the hidden person (see 1 Peter 3:4).

If we have been granted a certain amount of beauty, we need to thank God for it, in recognition that it has come from His good hands. It is a gift, and like all gifts should be properly used and cared for. But remember, external beauty is a fading gift.

For women who have not received the gift of physical beauty, I hope you are or can be free from this beauty idol. Exercise in your sweat pants, accept your body type, enjoy who you are, and remember that no matter how you look, you are still God's child. There are many today who are like the lame man lying outside the temple gate called Beautiful. Likewise, many women today feel they cannot enter at the Beauty gate because of their many flaws, scars, or deficiencies.

The solution for this lame individual was not surgery, but the Savior. The apostles told him "to walk in the name of Jesus" (Acts 3:1-8). He did. The man entered the gate called Beautiful and went into the temple compound. This is a picture of all those individuals who sit outside God's presence due to a flawed, imperfect, and sinful nature. In the same way Jesus healed the lame man, all of us who are imperfect can be healed by Jesus and made perfect in Him. He makes us all beautiful!

A young woman must realize that she enters into mature womanhood not by being the perfect 8 dress size, or by spending hours in her beauty routine, but by believing in Jesus Christ. She is perfect in Him and is without spot or blemish because of what He has done for her (see Ephesians 5:27).

But a young woman also needs to develop the ability to see beauty in even broader terms.

### Beauty Seen in Life's Events

As mentioned earlier in this chapter, one peril of the beauty myth is that it leads to rampant narcissism. A woman can get so caught up in her personal pursuit of beauty that she misses the beauty that may surround her every day. King Solomon had tasted all life could offer and from his experience drew some conclusions. One was that every life event gives some expression of beauty. He counsels, "He has made everything beautiful in its time" (Ecclesiastes 3:11, NIV).

This is good news for women. Knowing that the glory of the

young woman will fade one day, we can be reassured that at every phase of our journey (even old age), there will be some special beauty. Perhaps we need to slow down, and take the time we need to look for that special expression of beauty that might be within our eyesight right now. It might be just watching children play, or looking at a flower in full bloom, or thanking God for the beauty we *do* see in the mirror!

The second element of wisdom Solomon offers is that there is also a kind of beauty in just enjoying life: "Here is what I have seen to be good and fitting [beautiful]: to eat, to drink and enjoy oneself in all one's labor in which he toils under the sun" (Ecclesiastes 5:18). The anorectic woman thinks she is beautiful by not eating, but Solomon says there is a certain amount of beauty in eating and enjoying the good things God has allowed us to have.

From the biblical perspective, food is not an evil to be avoided. Paul tells the young man Timothy not to be an abstainer but an enjoyer of what God has given. Paul's reason is, "Everything created by God is good, and nothing is to be rejected, if it is received with gratitude; for it is sanctified by means of the word of God and prayer" (1 Timothy 4:4-5).

We need to take time to savor life's experiences, to enjoy every morsel that comes our way. Somehow, the deceiver has convinced us that sanctification (being a unique, whole individual) comes through bingeing, dieting, and exercising, rather than through thankfulness based on the Word of God. For the ones who have found the secret of seeing beauty in this much wider perspective, there is a freedom and joy about their lives. They have encountered a genuine spiritual beauty.

The choice is ours. Choices are brought about by forks in the road. On the young woman's journey, the issue of beauty is a fork in the road of her journey. The young woman must decide how she is going to view and use beauty in her life. She can choose to be an Esther or a Salome!

*A biblical portrait of two women: Salome and Esther*—Women who have regularly read the gospel stories have undoubtedly come across the rather obscure, unnamed daughter of Herodias (see Matthew 14:1-12, Mark 6:16-28). She was found performing at King Herod's birthday party, probably a fairly rowdy, drunken affair. From the Jewish historian Josephus we learn that her name was Salome.[30]

Herod Antipas, called Herod in the text, had a love-hate relationship with John the Baptist. He enjoyed listening to him preach. At the same time, due to John's very bold condemnation of the king's marriage to Herodias, his brother's ex-wife, Herod held a grudge against John.

John the Baptist condemned this union because it was a total violation of the Mosaic law, which prohibited the marriage of close relatives (see Leviticus 18:16, 20:21). Herod was both intrigued and perplexed by the unorthodox preacher. But Herodias was not as open-minded. She put pressure on Herod to have John jailed. Herod's birthday celebration became the guillotine for John. The blade was the power of a young woman's beauty—Salome (Herodias' daughter), the symbol of feminine power, beauty, and attractiveness to men.

The men were so overcome with her beauty that Herod decided he would impress his guests and offer Salome anything she wanted in return for her dancing. Salome was surprised by this offer and consults her mother. Herodias recognized very quickly that this was the opportunity she needed to eliminate the gadfly prophet locked in the dungeon. She told Salome, "Ask for the head of John the Baptist" (Mark 6:24).

The rest is history. Herod felt the tension between wanting to keep John alive because he was a righteous man and not wanting to lose face in front of his guests. In other words, the power of a beautiful young woman hooked Herod into doing what he didn't want to do. Herodias had used the power of her own daughter's beauty to accomplish what she wanted. Salome, perhaps not realizing the power of beauty she carried, allowed herself to be manipulated by both Herod and her mother.

Salome represents the negative power of beauty. In Esther we see the positive power of a young woman's beauty. Her story is told in the book of Esther.

Esther, a Jewish orphan, was raised by her cousin Mordecai in the empire of Persia. When the wife of the Persian king (probably Xerxes) fell out of favor with her husband because she refused to show up at one of his parties, the king began to look around for another queen. A beauty contest was proposed.

Upon entering the pageant, Esther was lavished with the finest of beauty treatments, six months with the oil of myrrh and six months with spices and cosmetics. When Esther appeared before King Xerxes, he was impressed and fell in love with her. Because of her beauty in form and face, she found a special kindness and favor in his eyes, enough to be given the royal crown.

At this point it would be easy to conclude that a young woman's beauty is the key to finding a man and gaining status. This is what happens sometimes, but the story of Esther immediately developed into a diabolical plot in which she became the heroine.

Haman, an arch rival against the Jews of Persia, planned to massacre them. Upon hearing of a decree that would mean the death of all Jews, Mordecai put on sackcloth and stood at the palace gates. Esther's maidens were informed, and they passed this information on to the queen. In a series of communiques back and forth, Mordecai finally told Esther, "Who knows whether you have not attained royalty for such a time as this?" (4:14).

In response, Esther asked all the Jews to pray and fast, apparently for her. She then took the initiative to appear uninvited before her husband, the king, an action that usually brought the sentence of death. She put on her finest royal apparel and stood before the throne to make a request. Again she found favor with her husband.

Esther used not only her beauty but her brains as she became the mediator for the lives of her people. After a series of palace incidents where God's providence was evident, Haman was hanged on his own gallows. Esther, the beauty-queen heroine, became the means of salvation for the Jewish people. She is still honored today during every festival of Purim.

The point illustrated here regarding a young woman's beauty is that of stewardship and contribution. A young woman's power lies in her beauty. Unfortunately, beauty can become her idolatrous god or her demon. Or it can be used to the glory of God, in service and contribution to His purposes. Like all God's gifts, the recipient can misuse or bury her talents or learn to use them in ways that will contribute to developing something more beneficial to herself and society.

In conclusion, the positive and negative consequences related to a woman's beauty, to whatever degree she has it, will accompany her continually along the feminine journey. They may bring her a sense of joy, satisfaction, and wholeness. Or they may bring her a sense of shame, dissatisfaction, and continual struggle. A woman's beauty can create for her new, challenging paths that make her life richer and fuller. On the other hand, a woman's beauty can also create distractions and limitations along the way.

Beauty is a gift of God and yet is manifested in so many ways. The concept of outward beauty changes like the tide and should be held lightly. Today's fashion is tomorrow's absurdity. As a woman travels through the various seasons of life, her perspective will change as to where her beauty lies. For some, it may be in her personality; for others, in her smile; and for others, in her sincerity or faithfulness.

Given enough time, only a hint of a woman's youthful beauty is evident. Yet, as the outer woman fades, the inner woman becomes stronger, her beauty radiating from the inside out. The older woman knows that the inner beauty of strength, perspective, and wisdom proves to be the most valuable and sustaining asset throughout her life: "Therefore, we do not lose heart, but though our outer man [woman] is decaying, yet our inner man [woman] is being renewed day by day" (2 Corinthians 4:16).

Hopefully, as a woman moves into the nurturing years of her life, her self-centered focus on beauty will be drawn outward. For the first time, the woman will, in most cases, be replaced as the center of her life by the precious creation of her own body, her child. By God's marvelous graciousness, He brings a woman out of her self-preoccu-pation and self-pleasure, and into the self-sacrificing season of the nurturing woman.

# CHAPTER FOUR

# THE NURTURER: THE MATERNAL MYSTIQUE

❦

*It seems to me I spent my life in car pools. But you know,*
*that's how I kept track of what was going on.*
**BARBARA BUSH**

*To have—to hold—and—in time--let go.*
**INDIA'S LOVE LYRICS**

Writing this book, *The Feminine Journey*, coincided with our second daughter, Ashley, leaving to attend college in Florida. I made a short trip with her in order to get her situated. Upon arriving home, I found myself lying on the bed in her room looking for traces of my middle child. The room certainly did not look the same as it had a few days ago. At that time, her clothes were strewn all over the room, her special music was playing on her CD player, and the smell of her perfume hung in the air.

This had been our last summer together. I had grabbed every moment I could as we went shopping, sat in the sun on the deck, or cooked her favorite oatmeal cookies. Even though the time had come for her to leave and be on her own, I felt the pain of this loss deeply within my heart.

As I think about this sweet child, I know that she is ready to face the world and she will survive whatever life throws at her. Isn't this the ultimate purpose of parenting, that we prepare our children to be mature adults ready to leave and make their mark in the world? The psalmist says, "Like arrows in the hand of a warrior, so are the children of one's youth. How blessed is the man [woman] whose quiver is full of them" (Psalm 127:4-5).

My quiver is now missing a second arrow as Ashley launches into the world of college. Bob and I have experienced the departure of our two daughters and now have only our sixteen-year-old son, Graham, still at home.

I entered motherhood twenty-four years ago, but it feels as if I've been a mother my entire life! This phase of my feminine journey has been a very rewarding season, and one I wouldn't have missed for the world.

My concept of nurturing changed throughout the years. I found myself periodically reevaluating my nurturing responsibilities as I took into account the changing needs and desires of the children as they matured. Many of you mothers might agree with me when I say now, at this point, I am most ready to be a mother. The reason may be, in part, that I have had to grow up first myself in some critical areas. All mothers probably grow up along with their children. This is what makes family relationships so challenging and interesting.

The concept of woman as a nurturer overflows into every area of life, not merely into parenting. Nurturing is considered to be a primarily feminine characteristic, although certainly not expressed only by women. Some men have a strong sense of caretaking, and some women may not feel naturally nuturing. Not all women desire to have children. That raises the question of whether nurturing is an inborn trait or an acquired one. I would suggest both beliefs are true, although differing in great degrees between the two sexes. Even when men nurture, they will do it distinctively as men.

The film *Three Men and a Baby* illustrates this classic difference. The movie is about a small baby who is dumped off with three bachelors, one of which is the biological father, so the mother can pursue her career. When the baby has an accident in her diaper while in a restaurant, the actor Ted Dansen takes the baby into the men's room to change her diaper. Realizing the bottom of the child is still damp, he awkwardly holds the baby up and looks around. Seeing the electric hand dryer on the wall, he proceeds to put the baby's bottom up to the dryer. When Bob and I saw this movie in the theater, women all around me in the audience gasped in shock. The men seemed to think it was a very logical thing to do!

The movie would be great for first-time parents to watch. It can give men (especially single men) an appreciation of how difficult it would be to care for a child on their own. It can give women an appreciation of their intuitive instincts for childcare as they witness the absurdities of the male mind in "creatively" caring for the child.

Women can also see that men usually lack this predisposition to meet a child's needs, causing women to value their innate nurturing ability to a greater degree. *Three Men and a Baby* ends with the single mother coming back for the baby and moving in with the three guys. One of the men responds by saying that the baby "needs a full-time mother."

It used to amaze me that Bob continually dressed the girls with their clothes on backwards. He could just never get it straight as to which was the front and which was the back. He said the problem was that the buttons are backwards on girls' and women's clothes, and he assumed everything buttoned in the front. Backwards from whose clothes?

## HOW MOMS ARE MADE

God commanded Adam and Eve to "be fruitful and multiply." The reproduction process involves both sexes for conception, but ultimately the woman is the primary player in the childbearing event. The New Testament Greek word for mother is *meter*, which is closely related to the Greek word *metra*, which means womb.

Within the mother's body, in the protected confines of the womb, the child will be nourished and grow until birth. When one thinks about the function of the womb, it is indeed one of the most illustrative aspects about what it means to be a womb-kind of man. The word *woman* is a derived from a combination of the old English words "womb" and "man."

The newly implanted embryo-child is connected to the mother inside the womb by means of the placenta. This marvelous structure allows a large variety of chemical and nutrient matter to be exchanged across the placental tissue between the developing child and the mother. Oxygen and carbon dioxide are exchanged here, allowing the child to live separately but connected with the mother. The mother's antibodies that protect the child are transferred to the child through the placenta, and the child's waste material is passed into the mother's bloodstream for removal.[1]

When the child is thrust into the world, the mother assumes the same "natural" responsibilities for the child that her womb did toward the unborn fetus. The same instincts of nourishing and protecting are as natural to the mother as the instincts of the womb.

These nurturing instincts are seen throughout the animal kingdom as well. When our beagle, Sadie, had puppies, she knew exactly what to do. She had not been to childbirth classes or prenatal care classes. She had a natural "puppy birth" and took great care of her pups until they were six to eight weeks old. It was amazing to observe Sadie, not only because she instinctively knew what to do when the puppies were born, but she also knew how to care for them as they grew. She knew when to wean them at the appropriate time and apparently had already "accepted" the fact that they would leave her to find new homes.

Of course people aren't animals. However, the same inherent nurturing instincts lie within the females of most species. It goes with the reproductive territory . . . and men don't have it!

Although the feminist agenda is committed to making sure women are granted equal rights in every area of life, there is one "right" (function) possessed by women that men don't have, and never will. Women *can* do one thing that men can never do. Feminist Carol Travis writes,

> A woman lawyer is exactly the same as a man lawyer. A woman cop is just the same as a man cop. And a pregnant woman is just the same as . . . well, as, uh . . . Pregnancy is just exactly like pregnancy! There is nothing else quite like it. That statement is not a glorification or a mystification. It is a statement of fact. Having a baby grow in your belly is not like anything else one can do. It is unique.[2]

Of course, we don't hear the men complaining. It is one area that clearly illustrates there are major differences in the genders by design. No amount of anger, infighting, manipulation, policies, or new laws can ever change this biological fact. A man cannot bear children. A man cannot be a mother. Not only is it biologically impossible, it is also emotionally and psychologically improbable.

Unfortunately, childbearing is also impossible for many women. Due to no fault of their own, medical problems, singleness, or divorce make childbearing impossible and in some cases, unwise. I bore three children quite easily and took it all very much for granted. As I reflect on how my life would have been without my children, I cannot even imagine it today. I cannot fully appreciate the depth of the struggles and feelings of frustration, deep sadness, and loss felt by those for whom childbearing will never be a reality.

To bear children and enter into this sacrificial, nurturing relationship is instinctive to most women. This instinct does not go away just because a woman finds her body unable to fulfill the process. I believe God has certain couples set aside to be either adoptive or foster parents, who are graced with the ability to love the children of others as their own. There are plenty of neglected and unloved children who need a nuturing touch or a welcoming home. God tells us in Isaiah 55:8, "For My thoughts are not your thoughts, neither are your ways My ways."

## THE NATURE OF NUTURING

Since the 1960s, there have been contradictory voices claiming to speak for all women concerning their desires and their rights. One commentator observed,

> Just at the moment when women are freest to enjoy and exploit their natural, superior skills in motherhood, a stern sisterhood tells them that this is an unnecessary, low-value and socially regressive role, predicting that the future will see the abolition of the traditional roles of parenthood, to be replaced with a communal Utopia.[3]

With the publication of *The Feminine Mystique* by Betty Freidan Pandora's box was opened in the area of women's issues. Women who were content to be at home and raise children were told that their place held no real value.

It was one thing to hear this subtle message from men. It was quite another matter suddenly to hear it from other women. The basic truth is that men will probably never place the same value on work at home as they do on work at the office because men value different things:

> It is only when women judge their own worth at men's evaluation that the problems arise. . . . Why should any woman consciously adopt a male value system which devalues her own female values? For a woman to try to be "more like a man" seems almost by definition to make her a less-happy woman.[4]

As much as some would like to believe that our desires are mere products of social conditioning or stereotypes, the nurturing characteristics of a woman are increasingly being recognized as a biological, emotional, and spiritual reality. It is true that women may differ in how they view their nurturing side. Many women today do choose careers in the working world over the experience of having children. For some, by the time they hear and acknowledge the small voice within them declaring their nurturing desires, the biological clock has wound down and it's too late.

Today, many career women, who opted out of motherhood in the eighties, are ready to embrace it in the nineties. We are told that the number of women over forty who are bearing their first child doubled between 1984 and 1988: "A growing number of unmarried adult single women adopt or give birth to children. In 1989 more than 100,000 children were born to unwed mothers age thirty to thirty four—more than six times the 1979 number. In both years thirty percent had some college education."[5]

Why do women hear this inner voice? Men may have the "out-of-nowhere" urge to get married, but it is usually prefaced by other events such as meeting the girl of their dreams or finally realizing that all their friends are married. With most women it is different. The nurturing instinct seems to be at the core of our being. This instinct is a critical aspect of what it means to be a woman. It is, perhaps, one of the most natural stages on the feminine journey.

The aspect of nurturing does not have to be restricted exclusively to the area of motherhood. As women we take a nurturing approach to most of our relationships. Just as studies have shown that men characteristically approach life from the perspectives of hierarchy, detachment, power, and one-upmanship, so women approach life as nurturers.[6] This seems to be the case whether they are housewives, secretaries, businesswomen, or military officers.

Changes in the world of business have brought a change in management style. As the authors of *Reinventing the Corporation* wrote, "Now in the information society, as the manager's role shifts to that of the teacher, mentor, and nurturer of human potential, there is even more reason for corporations to take advantage of women's managerial abilities, because these people-oriented traits are the ones women are socialized to possess."[7] Women bring to the workplace a "nurturing" style of leadership that is referred to as "empowerment."[8] This nurturing leadership style is "the ability to maximize the contributions of others by helping them to effectively guide their own destinies, rather than the ability to bend the will of others to the leaders."[9]

Bob serves as chaplain in the Air National Guard. He is often asked about his views on women in the military. His standard reply is that they have brought a very needed perspective into the military community. Even though he does not believe a battlefield is a place for any human being, much less women, he has been very favorably impressed by the professionalism, dedication, and skills women have brought to the job. When I asked him what *most* characterizes what women have brought to the military community, he said without hesitation, "Their caring perspective." Many may disagree that women should be in the military or in combat roles. However, when they do show up, what they bring with them—married or not, mothers or not—are the elements of caring and nurturing.

It is affirming for women to know that there is much within their nurturing and relational nature (which will be discussed in the next chapter) that effectively equips them for leadership in the workplace. What comes naturally as well as skills learned through the school of motherhood and homemaking make women well-prepared for leadership in whatever field is chosen.

Where does this nurturing instinct begin? The psalmist says very clearly that all of us have our unique identities, including gender, "knit together" in the womb: "For you created my inmost being; you knit me together in my mother's womb" (Psalm 139:13, NIV). If we can go back to Biology 101 or the course we took in college on Human Sexuality, we find the amazing "miracle" that took place at the very beginning of the formation of little boys and girls. For girls, our development as nurturers begins in the womb. In *Brain Sex*, Anne Moir and David Jessel point out:

> It is not until six or seven weeks after conception the unborn baby "makes up its mind," and the brain begins to take on a male and female pattern. What happens at that critical stage in the darkness of the womb will determine the structure and organization of the brain: and that, in turn will decide the very nature of the mind. It is one of the most fascinating stories of life and creation; a story largely unknown, but now, at last, beginning to unfold in its entirety.
>
> We have known some of the story for some time. We know that the genes, carrying the coded blueprint of our unique characteristics, make us either male or female. In every microscopic cell of our bodies, men and women are different from each other; because every fibre of our being has a different set of chromosomes within it, depending on whether we are male or female.[10]

The mother contributes an X chromosome within her egg, while the father can contribute either an X or a Y chromosome through his sperm. If the father's contribution is another X chromosome, the offspring will be a girl; if a Y chromosome, then the outcome will be a little boy. Each partner contributes twenty-three chromosomes to the package, making up in the normal human, forty-six chromosomes.

We have learned that the presence or absence of hormones, even in varying amounts, is also critically important. While recognizing the role of environment and socialization, hormones have a certain "programing" effect on later development. The more male hormone the fetus is exposed to, the more the adult will be male in behavior; in lesser amounts, the more feminine the adult behavior. For women, this means that the lack of high testosterone levels and the presence of estrogen (female hormone) account for significant differences. Another researcher notes:

> The differences between estrogen and testosterone are still being investigated. Basically, we know that testosterone is a male hormone responsible for a number of effects, including aggression, competition, deeper and more forceful voices, hair coarseness, and the like. Estrogen is a roller-coaster hormone that affects mood changes (PMS), fat storage, and egg production. The effects of estrogen cannot be predicted as easily as testosterone.
>
> As noted earlier, the woman's immune system (because of the XX chromosome) functions at a higher level than a man's. The female immune system is so efficient that it sometimes attacks the body it is supposed to protect. Women suffer much more than men from autoimmune diseases.
>
> Mother Nature protects women for the purpose of motherhood, whether or not as individuals they want to have children. Men are genetically programed to be hunters and sex-seekers, whether or not as individuals they hunt or seek sex. Estrogen and progesterone give women that "glow," self-assurance, and readiness for procreation.[11]

It would seem, then, that in every cell of a woman's body, lies this basic maternal-nurturing characteristic. The maternal approach to life, relationships, even work, is unique to her being. This nurturing aspect is not only a major stage on a woman's journey, but it is also a part of her that stays with her the entire trip. However, in the past few

decades, women for differing reasons have been resisting and reject-
ing outright this fundamental aspect of their natures.


## WE FORGET TO HAVE KIDS

Bob still remembers having to read *The Population Bomb*, by Paul
Ehrlich, when he was in college. It was required reading for a fresh-
man biology class. The premise of the book was that the world was
facing the severe threat of overpopulation. This problem was thrown
into the mix with other global difficulties such as international conflict, violence, famine, economic problems and poverty. The bottom
line was that to be responsible human beings, we should limit childbearing. Some argued that it was "cruel" to bring into this world
another human being who was only going to further devour the planet.
The book was a best seller, and apparently Americans took it seriously
and began limiting the number of children born per household.

Today some scholars are beginning to realize that either the bomb
did not go off or it just fizzled out. However, the result is clear. Our
birth rate has dropped significantly. In the very first American census
done in 1790, the completed fertility rate was seven children per
couple. "Completed" fertility meant the average woman had more
children than seven, but only seven lived to adulthood. So the actual
number of children born was higher. By 1890, the rate had dropped to
four children. In 1990, the fertility rate plunged to an all-time low of
1.7 children.[12]

Obviously, both parents eventually die. In order to have just a
replacement population, the birth rate must be at least 2.1, because
some children will die.

What are the consequences of a low birth rate? Doesn't this mean
having less people to feed and employ will make for better living conditions among those who are here? Ben Wattenberg of the American
Enterprise Institute in Washington D.C. disagrees:

> During the last 300 years, when economic progress in the world
> was most explosive, there was enormous population growth in
> those nations where the most vigorous economic system (capital-
> ism) was most potent and prevalent. Let us put a little recent
> American flesh on these numbers.
>
> What did it mean in practice in America? Well, for one, there
> was always plenty of fresh demand for more housing.

Accordingly, if an individual or a company was in the business of building or selling residences—from slums to penthouses—in Connecticut or California—there was almost always a demand for more residences. If a person grew or sold or processed food or fiber—grain or granola, cotton or silk—there was almost always a demand for more food or fiber. If a company built or sold cars—Model T's or El Dorados—there was almost always a demand for more cars. If a company designed, manufactured, distributed, or sold word processors or personal computers—IBMs or Apples—there was almost always a demand for more of them. If a company sold fast food—Wendy's or Taco Bell—there was almost always more people to buy the burgers or the burritos. More. Always more.

The scenario is ending. The Western world—our world—is already moving from a situation of fast growth to slow growth. A no-growth circumstance is already in the deck. There will be actual declines in most Western nations unless there are important changes in fertility levels fairly soon.[13]

In short, a low fertility rate makes for fewer young workers entering the economy, who will also be buyers of products. They are also the ones who will to pay into Social Security to support you and me! As Wattenberg says, "We don't put money into Social Security for our own pensions. We put in babies!"[14]

I wonder how many women have failed to listen to our nurturing natures and for whatever reasons have contributed to the 1.7 fertility rate. What is most alarming about our nation's "birth dearth" is that we have done it to ourselves. Our low fertility rate is not due to the common causes seen throughout history: war, famine, and disease. Ours is entirely self-imposed, reflecting our values (or non-values) and philosophy of life. Why did we not have children or have more children or abort the ones we did have? Was it inconvenient, too expensive, too much of a constriction on our lifestyle? Did we really buy into the population bomb myth?

There is a gripping poster I have seen several times. It shows an attractive, white female, with her hand covering most of her face. From her uncovered eye, a tear is beginning to run down her cheek. The caption on the poster reads: "I Can't Believe It. I Forgot to Have Children."

We must not apologize for being what we are as women. We have been formed from day one of our existence to be nurturers. In a 1985 Virginia Slims/Harris survey, over 90 percent of all American young women said they wanted to get married and have children.[15] Contrary socialization during the past several decades has not changed the fundamental nature of women. Even while training for and engaged in professional careers, women feel the maternal urge. I don't think it should be denied or denigrated.

## THE BIBLICAL NURTURER

It seems even in biblical times, the pendulum swung from over-regard toward motherhood as illustrated in the "mother cults," to the under-regard for motherhood that was characteristic at several points in both Israel's history and that of the pagan world. In an extended summary detailing the Hebrew and Greek terms for "mother" during biblical times, Beyreuther writes:

> A high estimation of motherhood and parenthood can be traced everywhere in antiquity. Already in pre-historic times (This is shown by numerous finds of small images of expectant mothers with pronounced sexual characteristics), man was aware of the close relationship between human life and that of the earth itself. The earth became the great mother who gives everything and then in death takes everything back into herself. Thus, in many regions the oldest figures of the gods are earth mothers (cf. mother earth, "mater terra, magna mater").
>
> Such mother-deities which are represented anthropomorphically, play a great part in the popular religions of the East. Veneration of them often led to cultic prostitution, in order to gain an immediate share in their life-controlling powers, as in the Canaanite cult of Astarte. Yet, the picture of the mother-deity can also be spiritualized and civilized and be detached from the highly erotic domain of the figure of Venus, as in the case of the Egyptian goddess, Isis, the embodiment of the true wife and mother. On the other hand it can assume the cruel and bloody traits of an Artemis or a Kali. We find in the mother-deities the whole gamut of female possibilities.[16]

Never before has there been more confusion for women concerning their responsibilities in the home. Contemporary women have torn up the blueprint of past roles and stereotypes, yet seem to struggle for some map and guidance. The drive for career success and achievement in the working world has resulted in some women sabotaging their own biological and emotional makeup. As Christians, it is important to rediscover God's blueprint for the nurturing woman in motherhood. Contrary to modern views, which have devalued this position and its impact on the lives of children, the biblical admonitions and illustrations present a much different viewpoint.

## MOTHERHOOD IS HIGHLY REGARDED

Adam and Eve led humankind from a position of blessedness and oneness with each other, God, and the earth to a position of separation between themselves and from God. Through their disobedience, the perfect picture of creation was marred. There was conflict now between man and his mate and man and his environment. However, God had a plan for the redemption of man and began this plan with the woman.

Prior to the Fall, Adam had been named but the woman was unnamed. She was called "*ishah*," which showed a gender difference from the man. However, after the Fall, Adam called the woman "Eve" (*hawwa*), which means "living" or "life-giver," or as stated in the text "the mother of all the living" (Genesis 3:20). One commentary suggests that this "signifies that the woman became a pledge in the continuation of the race, in spite of the curse. The name celebrates the survival of the race and the victory over death. By anticipating life, it also commemorates the establishment of a new order."[17]

Adam and Eve accepted their circumstances, and despite everything, Adam's faith is revealed through the name he gives the woman. Eve symbolizes the continuing life of a couple and of the entire human race. Satan was not victorious, and through the woman would come both his ultimate destruction and salvation for humankind. Children are always the promise of the future. Without women and children there would be no future for men. Protecting the women and children was critically important to the Jewish nation. Many times they were caught in the middle of harmful situations that had been created by the conflicts and chaos of sinful men who took no account of the impact of their misguided or evil actions on the lives of innocents.

One such account occurs when Jacob is attempting reconciliation with his brother, Esau. Jacob had manipulated his father into bestowing upon him the blessing that Esau should have had as oldest son. After years of anger, fear, and separation, Jacob seeks a reunion with Esau. At this point, Jacob has accumulated much wealth with many wives and children. His greatest fear as Esau approaches his camp is that the mothers and the children of his extended family will be destroyed. Jacob reminds God that if he loses his family, he will lose his posterity, for they are his personal hope in the promises of God (Genesis 32:11-12).

Motherhood is to be honored according to the Fifth Commandment (see Exodus 20:12). As I understand it, this is a lifelong command. Children are to obey parents only as long as they are children, but even adult children are still to honor and respect their parents for life. Scripture also condemns any treatment or perspective that seeks to despise, attack, shame, or sexually abuse those who give life (see Leviticus 19:3; Proverbs 15:20, 19:26).

In passage after passage in the books of 1 and 2 Kings and 1 and 2 Chronicles, each king of Israel mentioned is listed with his mother's name. This is a seemingly rare and unusual custom, since in biblical Jewish circles, the lineage is traced through the father, not the mother. Kings are listed as sons of their mothers. That's a high tribute to the mothers (see 2 Kings 11–24, 2 Chronicles 12–29).

When the prophet Jeremiah describes how God's judgment is going to fall upon the nation of Israel, he paints the dark portrait of a nation without its mothers and children (see Jeremiah 15:5-10). The depiction here could be equally true of the Western world today, but who is weeping? Where are our weeping prophetic voices, lamenting the loss of mothers because they were never born, or the loss of children through violence and abortion?

Throughout the Old Testament the mother's nurturing responsibilities are of primary importance, as seen in their care and character building of children. Hagar and Naomi take the initiative in finding spouses for their children (see Genesis 21:21, Ruth 3:1-5). The marriage covenant was considered so important that both the mother and the father would be involved in assuring the sexual purity of their daughter, whether by protecting her rights or participating in her punishment (see Deuteronomy 22:13-21).

In typical maternal fashion, mothers are observed taking care of the physical provisions for their families in both food preparation and clothing (see 1 Samuel 2:19; Proverbs 31:13-15,18-19).

During the early years of our marriage, when money was tight due to Bob's years in graduate school, we were challenged to be very creative in providing for the needs of our children in the areas of food and clothing. I could pull out the sewing machine, being grateful for my ninth grade home economics class, and begin sewing for the girls.

I wasn't the best seamstress then, and today my sewing machine collects dust. But I look back with fond memories on the fun of making my children's clothes. It was a learning experience for me and gave me a great sense of pride in my somewhat limited abilities.

Food preparation was truly a challenge during those financially lean times. I remember the encouragement of reading Edith Schaffer's book *Hidden Art*. Her book gave me a vision and encouragement for making even the simplest meals attractive and fun. Not too long ago, while I was shopping with my daughter, Ashley, buying food for her new apartment, she noticed the Spam sitting next to the tuna fish on the shelf. She said, "What is this stuff, and do people really eat it?"

I laughed as memories suddenly flooded my mind. "Honey," I chuckled, "Spam was occasionally the main course for our evening meal when your dad was in graduate school." Fortunately, she didn't remember those days and just shook her head in amazement.

On the other hand, our oldest daughter, Charis, vividly remembers some of those meager meals. Interestingly enough, she is now married to a minor league baseball player, and their financial situation is similar to ours in the early days of marriage. She will never let me forget the time we didn't have any bread in the house for a few days, and I had to send her to nursery school with peanut butter and pancake sandwiches. Now she is making the best of their situation and finds comfort in the fact that we lived through it and survived!

Unfortunately today, many young people have been raised in affluent times, and now that the economy is tighter they have no background or history in knowing how to "tighten the belt." Whether they appreciated it at the time or not, our children have experienced having to trust God not only for food but for other significant "needs" like college tuition. Often, the provision has come about very creatively.

A mother's opportunity to teach her children the reality of how to trust in God's provisional care is one of the most important influences she can have. From the moment a child enters into life, the trusting relationship with its mother is one of the most critical. We hope that as the child matures this trust will one day transfer from the mother to one's heavenly Father. Of course, both parents are critical in establishing a trust relationship with the child. But it is the mother who has the initial nurturing contact with the child, creating a unique mother-child bond.

The proverbs reiterate time and again that the mother's teachings are the framework around which the life of the child grows (Proverbs 1:8, 6:20, 31:1). The opportunities a mother has to teach are so numerous simply because of the amount of time mother and child spend together throughout each day. Today, with so many mothers of young children working, one must raise the question of who is now developing the character of the children. We all realize daycare centers, baby-sitters, and other outside influences have now taken over this responsibility. For many single mothers, there are no other options. But one wonders whether the next generation of children, without the necessary time for bonding and trust to develop between mother and child, will be able to trust anyone, let alone God.

Our society today is so concerned about all the special interest groups' rights. However, for the most part, these are all adult groups that have legal options for declaring and demanding their rights. But as a society we seem very confused when it comes to the rights and needs of our children. Some politicians and attorneys "seem" to be fighting for children's rights by granting parental authority to government. Do they really understand the needs of children? Or is this the dangerous result of political ideology?

More power and responsibility are being stripped from the hands of the parents. Unfortunately, so many parents today did not receive proper parenting, and they are passing on to their children dysfunctional attitudes and behavior patterns. The breakdown of the American family, the hurried pace of our technological age, and the eclectic smorgasbord of values leave our children unprotected and confused.

The impact of a changing society on our children and teenagers has been most effectively addressed by child psychologist Dr. David Elkind, author of *The Hurried Child* and *All Grown Up and No Place to Go*. In *The Hurried Child* he wrote:

> Today's child has become the unwilling, unintended victim of
> overwhelming stress—the stress borne of rapid, bewildering
> social change and constantly rising expectations. The contempo-
> rary parent dwells in a pressure-cooker of competing demands,

transitions, role changes, personal and professional uncertainties, over which he or she exerts slight direction. We seek release from stress whenever we can, and usually the one sure gambit of our control is the home. Here if nowhere else, we enjoy the fact (or illusion) of playing a determining role. If child-rearing necessarily entails stress, then by hurrying children to grow up or by treating them as adults, we hope to remove a portion of our burden of worry and anxiety and to enlist our children's aid in carrying life's load. We do not mean our children harm in acting thus—on the contrary, as a society we have come to imagine that it is good for young people to mature rapidly. Yet, we do our children harm when we hurry them through childhood.[18]

Every journey needs a map. The journey from childhood to the teen years and into adulthood are today hurried and confused. For this trip there's not much guidance. There is a need for mothers and fathers to stand in the gap and both protect their children as well prepare them for the journey ahead.

Bob writes about the "warrior" stage of a man's journey as it relates to his struggles and accomplishments in the workplace. Women, too, have this warrior instinct to fight for what is theirs. We have witnessed the strength of this instinct expressed by women in the feminist movement in their struggle for women's equal rights. My question is, Why have we not seen this warrior instinct expressed by women who are concerned about the protection of their homes and their children? History reveals a woman's power can be used mightily for either good purposes, resulting in the preservation of her nation, or for evil purposes, resulting in the destruction of the nation.

Deborah, a prophetess of Israel during the time of the judges, was a strong representative of this "warrior woman." While "the sons of Israel did evil in the sight of God" (Judges 4:1), the Israelites were captured by the Canaanite military commander, Sisera. Deborah's leadership and courageous faith earned her the position of a judge, or political/military leader, during this critical time. Through her direction and gutsy faith, God used Deborah to defeat the Canaanite army. At the same time, God used another courageous woman, Jael, to drive a peg through the skull of Sisera. These were tough women fighting for their God, their nation, and their children. The result was that peace reigned in the land for forty years. Deborah even composed a song of tribute to their victory and God's faithfulness. Not bad for a wife and mother! She may be an ancient model of the current working mothers (see Judges 4–5), but here she worked for the sake of her children and her nation.

Jezebel illustrates the opposite power, the power of an evil woman with negative influences. Jezebel was the daughter of a Canaanite king from the city of Sidon. She had been raised in a pagan culture that worshiped Baal and the goddess Ashtoreth. The worship of Baal was associated with lascivious rites and the sacrifice of children. In this ritual, parents would throw their own children into blazing fires in order to bring blessing upon their lives and crops.

When King Ahab married Jezebel, she influenced her husband toward evil, and together they brought Baal worship into Samaria: "Thus Ahab did more to provoke the Lord, God of Israel, than all the kings of Israel who were before him" (1 Kings 16:33).

The list of Jezebel's sins is legion. Her evil influence brought about the death of most of the prophets of the Lord, except for Elijah. After her death, the evil influence of Jezebel remained in her son, Ahaziah. His reign as king over Israel in Samaria lasted for two years. Scripture alludes to the impact of his mother in this short passage: "He did evil in the sight of the Lord and walked in the way of his father and in the way of his mother. . . . So he served Baal and worshiped him and provoked the LORD God of Israel to anger according to all that his father had done" (1 Kings 22:52-53).

Think of how many individuals are in counseling today, "working through issues" with their mothers (and fathers). The stamp a mother leaves on her children for good or evil is recognized in Scripture as a uniform principle. The prophet Ezekiel decries the sins of Israel's idolatry and harlotry as he likens her to a then contemporary proverb: "Like mother, like daughter"—if the mother hated her husband and children, so will her daughter (Ezekiel 16:44). A painful reality, but one we mothers must face. Our influence is significant.

But there are some other realities we must also face.

## REALITIES OF MOTHERHOOD

The pleasures of motherhood are the greatest we experience. Likewise, the pains of motherhood leave wounds and hurts we carry for a lifetime. Even though women are endowed with the biological equipment to bear children, not all women are blessed with a personal background or positive childhood experiences to equip them emotionally or psychologically to raise healthy children. This handicap is often not apparent until a woman is actually in the process of raising children. Often we hear stories on the news about the abuse or death of a child at the hands of the mother. We find this almost impossible to comprehend and yet it does happen.

The fact remains that most mothers, at one point or another, get pushed beyond their limits and find themselves, out of anger or frustration, crossing the line from nurturer to aggressor. We lash out and say something cruel and unkind to our child. Worse, we may strike a child, knowing immediately that we don't want to do this but can't help ourself.[19] Most of the time, we are able to gain control, acknowledge and learn from our mistakes, and try to remember what we have learned about ourself. Others may eventually see that their own inappropriate and harmful treatment of the child is beyond their control, and seek help.

Society has a black-and-white view of motherhood, with a tendency to either idealize it or devalue it. A mother is considered either "good" or "bad." The reality is that we are neither one or the other. Sometimes our mothering techniques are "good," and other times they are "bad." Motherhood not only exposes the depth of our love, hopes, and abilities, but it also exposes the darker side of our personal unmet needs and childhood pains.

In her book *The Myth of the Bad Mother*, psychologist Jane Swigart describes the paths of this parenting journey. She suggests,

> Whether we are male or female, parents or childless, the care of children reawakens our buried selves. For better or worse, child care pulls us in two directions: outward toward the children we tend and inward toward our own earliest experiences of being cared for. Our first, most intense relationship with our mother often remains unconscious and inaccessible until we have children, at which point all the longings and ambivalence we felt toward her rise up in us again.[20]

For those of us with a positive childhood experience, motherhood is an opportunity to reenact those wonderful, loving years when we felt loved, valued, and cared for. For those of us who remember mainly painful childhood experiences, we may enter parenthood thinking we will make it different for our children. However, often raising children draws us back into these painful experiences. We may have to relive some traumatic events or feelings that have been denied deep within the hidden recesses of our mind. The woundedness of childhood affects every area of our lives, not only our sense of what nurturing should look like.

One mother shared this sad realization about her childhood with me: "It was not until I experienced love for my own children that I realized my parents really didn't love me. It was very painful for me to acknowledge this truth and examine its impact on my life. It took extensive counseling and a very patient husband while I worked this out."

The good news is that we share the imperfections of motherhood with countless numbers of women throughout history. The Scriptures are full of well-meaning mothers who made wrong decisions concerning their children. Sarah's impatience in waiting for God's promise of an heir resulted in the exile of an innocent woman and her son, and eventually the creation of an adversarial nation (see Genesis 16:15, 17:20, 21:21). The scheming, half-truth pattern of Sarah and Abraham was passed to their son, Isaac (see Genesis 26). Rebekah was chosen by God to marry Isaac, and her son Jacob is recorded in the lineage of Christ. Yet Rebekah's favoritism between her twin boys, Jacob and Esau, and her lack of faith in God's promise for Jacob's future created a tremendous chasm between her sons (see Genesis 24–25). Despite the imperfections seen both in biblical characters and all humankind, God continues to extend His grace and care for His creatures.

Motherhood requires a quality of love that surpasses one's finite ability. It demands self-sacrifice, and possibly setting aside one's personal career goals. It means meeting the exhausting demands of both the physical and emotional needs of the child, with little appreciation and gratitude from not only family members but society as a whole. Then there is the pain of loss and aloneness when the child inevitably leaves home.

Another reality of motherhood is that good mothers can raise bad children and bad mothers can raise good children. This is a principle none of us likes to face. It so blows our categories, and takes away the power we feel we have as mothers. Some mothers have done the best they could with their children—sacrificing their own personal plans, going to all the school meetings, taking them to church, meeting their physical needs, and then feel like a failure when the child does not live up to mom's expectations. A daughter you loved and held such dreams for is now pregnant out of wedlock. Your son, who was given all the advantages, ends up in jail on drug charges. You gave your child the best you had and now feel betrayed, grief-stricken, and ashamed (see Proverbs 10:1, 29:15). You took your childrin to church, you prayed for them, and trusted God for their well-being. So what happened?

During the crisis, two responses seem imperative. First is to maintain the perspective that your child is still in a developmental process. As the child grows, you cannot control the harmful choices that he or she may make, or the painful consequences. Cling to the truth that God is in control and still loves you and your child.

Second, remember that your heavenly Father is well acquainted with wandering, erring, rebellious children. Both the nation of Israel and the church have caused Him immeasurable sorrow. Philip Yancy points this out in *Disappointment With God*: "Rejection is what God experienced not just from one child but from the entire human race."[21] Even God was not spared the difficulties of parenting. He will not always spare us this hardship. However, He alone is able to redeem the sorrows, supply comfort, and accompany us through our valley of pain.

Human beings come with no guarantees. At some point, mothers and fathers must realize that the ultimate future of their children lies in God's hands and the child's adult choices. Even Solomon alludes to the reality that parents can only encourage in a certain direction, but ultimately the choice is the child's. All the admonitions in Proverbs 2:1-9 are conditional, subject to the child responding positively.

This painful area may be the greatest testing ground for a parent's faith throughout life's journey. As we stand back and look at our children, there is either the tendency to swell with pride over our accomplishment or shrink back in shame over the apparent shambles of our child's life. In both cases (unless the child has died), the story is still not over. One never knows what events life will throw at our children or what unforseen trigger will change their course. In either case, do not be overly confident or totally in despair.


## A BIBLICAL PORTRAIT: MARY, THE MOTHER OF JESUS

Mary certainly could not have predicted the course her Son's life would take. Her feminine journey through motherhood, although unique in regards to the nature of her Son Jesus illustrates many of the experiences of all mothers.

Mary's journey began with an unusual pregnancy, unique in terms of conception, and laced with the social stigma of being an unwed mother. The particulars may have changed, but many women enter motherhood under difficult circumstances and travel down a rough and rocky road. Today's influences, freedoms, and changing societal values have resulted in more and more unwed women becoming pregnant. For those who value the sanctify of life and choose not to terminate their pregnancy, this can be a challenging time. It is our hope that strength can be derived from relatives and friends. As one apparently seeking outside support, Mary found it in her cousin, Elizabeth. Elizabeth provided the divine perspective on Mary's "situation," which allowed Mary to continue on the road to motherhood.

After the birth of Jesus, we have occasional glimpses into His specialness. The proclamations of the magi and the shepherds, the presentation of Jesus at the temple with the prophet Simeon, and Anna's prophecies were all special events that began to paint a portrait for Mary of the life of her Son. "Jesus kept increasing in wisdom and stature, and in favor with God and men" (Luke 2:52).

Then the time came for Mary and Joseph, as it does for all parents, when the adolescent child begins his move toward independence. At the age of twelve, Jesus stayed behind in the temple in Jerusalem communicating with the rabbis, while Mary and Joseph made their way home. As Jesus was rebuked by His parents for causing them concern, He began to open the door to what lay ahead for them as parents. He was about his "Father's business." Jesus was beginning to separate from His parents, a very critical task if He was to be the Man God purposed Him to be.

A mother's intuition is strong. Our knowledge and observations of our child are usually keener than those of the father. As the primary care-giver, the mother makes it her business to be aware. Mary took mental pictures of the growing-up years of her Son and "treasured all these things in her heart" (Luke 2:51).

The other day as I was cleaning our bedroom, my eyes landed on a pile of photographs stuffed in a box under the dresser. I intended to take only a couple of minutes to look at a few pictures as I moved the box to vacuum. However, one hour later I was still sitting on the floor, totally surrounded by photographs, and absolutely lost in my memories of events and people that seemed so far removed in another lifetime, but now so real again in the discovered photos. Was that young woman holding her newborn really me over twenty years ago?

Throughout Mary's life she must have found joy and comfort in the "mental photographs" of her nurturing years. There are only two more events recorded in Scripture pertaining to Mary's relationship with her Son, Jesus. Bible scholars suggest that since Joseph is unmentioned throughout the adult life and ministry of Jesus, he must have died.[22] Both the wedding at Cana (John 2:1-11) and the public teaching ministry of Jesus with the multitudes (Matthew 12:46-50) illustrate the progressive separation Jesus made from His family. On both occasions, Mary assumed her "mothering" role and tried to influence Jesus to do what she wanted. It is so common for mothers, as they try to adjust to their maturing children, occasionally to slip back into the "nurturing" role. Such may have been Mary's compulsion. Nevertheless, Jesus made it very clear that His relationship with His mother had changed. This is clearly revealed when He called Mary "woman" instead of "Mother" at the wedding, indicating a new distance and definition of the relationship. Jesus no longer belonged primarily to Mary. He was the Son of God.

The greatest pain a woman can experience at this nurturing stage is that of letting go. Of course, it is imperative and natural that the child separate in order to mature and establish his own identity apart from the mother. It starts to take place in adolescence and is usually accompanied by a certain amount of anger and resentment toward the mother's care and attention. The smartest and least painful response for the mother is finally to cut the umbilical cord.

What this means is letting the child assume the responsibility for his own life and then being there for support and guidance when asked. It may also mean being there to give perspective when things don't work out for the fallen teen. Unfortunately, many of us take this "rejection" personally and seek to hold on tighter. One of Bob's seminary professors, Howard Hendricks, used to say, "Whenever you do something for your child that your child is capable of doing for himself, you are developing an emotional cripple." Wise words indeed!

Mary followed Jesus throughout His ministry and was there whenever He needed her. Her nurturing journey with her Son eventually led her to the foot of the cross. This could not have been the plan she would have devised for her Son. As a mother, I'm sure I would have done anything to prevent its reality. However, Mary had fulfilled her nurturing role with her Son. I am sure, as she stood there at the cross for hours, surrounded by the hostile, laughing multitudes, Mary's thoughts journeyed back through the childhood years, reliving the joys, digging up the treasured mental photos so deliberately stored in her heart.

Her pain and suffering were those of all mothers for all time, pain only a mother can uniquely experience. As she examined the agony in His eyes, she yearned to reach out and soothe the wounds inflicted on His body, the same body of the baby she had cuddled, nursed, and cared for those many years before. As Mary had shared in the ecstasy of His birth, so she shared in the agony of His death.

Amid the agony of crucifixion, Jesus looked upon the multitudes along the hillside. So many faces, so much noise, such a stench of death, such great pain. It truly was Golgotha, the place of the skull! And yet, as He looked down, there she was. She was always there, whenever He needed her . . . His mother.

He had to know both the depth of her suffering and her love (see John 2:24). Earlier in His life, He had set her apart for a while in order to be about His Father's business. In these final moments Jesus reached out to the mother He loved. He touched her with the love of His eyes and the tenderness of His voice. Mary had cared for Him; now He would care for her. It was the custom for the oldest son to make provision for the care of his mother in her old age. Jesus had not forgotten. He said, "Woman, behold, your son" (John 19:26).

These few words meant so much to Mary. She might have heard, "Thank you for being My mother. Thank you for all the loving care you gave to Me as your Son. Thank you for so liberally sharing Me with the world, not only in life but now in My death. I know it wasn't easy and there is much you do not understand. You did not know that it was all in preparation for this. I love you."

To John, the faithful disciple, the one whom Jesus loved, and the only disciple at the cross, He said, "Behold, your mother" (John 19:27). Jesus told John to consider Mary as he would his own mother and care for her the remaining days of her life.

Then Jesus died. As the soldier's sword pierced Jesus' side, confirming His death, the sword also pierced Mary to her very soul. At this point, she did not know that three days later she would be a witness to the resurrection and final ascension of Jesus into Heaven. All she knew was that the painful death of her Son had reached the depths of her soul. Would life ever be the same again?

Many mothers, like Mary, find their nurturing years end in tragedy and pain through the death of a child. Bob and I have walked with several parents through this grief process after the unexpected deaths of children. It is a pain like no other pain. There is something about the death of a child or young person that catches everyone off guard.

It seems like such a violation of what should be. Everything in you screams in anger and frustration, "This isn't right! This isn't the way God meant it to be!" There are no answers to explain the death of a child. As one mother put it after the death of her little girl, "I wasn't through being a mother yet. It's hard for me to accept my days of mothering are over."

The death of a child, no matter what the age, turns this nurturing stage into a sad failure for many, and the complete antithesis of what mothering is all about. Dr. Theresa Rando wrote in her book, *Grieving*,

> With the death of your child you have failed in the basic function of parenthood; taking care of the children and the family. You are supposed to protect and provide for your child. You are supposed to keep her from all harm. She should be the one who grows up healthy to bury you.
>
> When you "fail" at this, when your child dies, you may feel that you have failed at your most basic function.
>
> The death of any child is a monumental assault on your sense of identity. Because you cannot carry out your role of preserving your child, you may experience an oppressive sense of failure, a loss of power and ability, and a deep sense of being violated. Disillusionment, emptiness, and insecurity may follow, all of which stem from a diminished sense of self. And this can lead to the guilt which is such a common feature in parental grief.[23]

Many of us, by some miracle, have had an overall positive experience in this nurturing phase of our journey. We rejoice in the lives of our children, accepting their ups and downs, and feel somewhat relieved when our role as primary caregiver is at an end (see Proverbs 23:24-25). Our feelings of relief are often mixed with tinges of regret and loss. As a woman continues through her feminine journey, certain pains of woundedness plague and torment every area of her life.

However, not all of a woman's wounds are related to her nurturing years. Many of the pains we face are the result of just living in an imperfect world filled with tragedies, difficulties, a variety of losses, illness, and ultimately death. As difficult as these experiences are, they, too, are an inescapable part of our feminine journey.

# CHAPTER FIVE

# THE RELATIONAL WOMAN: UNIQUELY FEMININE

❦

*What a woman thinks of women is*
*the test of her nature.*
GEORGE MEREDITH
*DIANA OF THE CROSSWAYS*

*The two kinds of people on earth that I mean*
*Are the people who lift and the people who lean.*
ELLA W. WILCOX
*TO LIFT OR LEAN*

$M$y twin sister and I planned a "girls only" time with our mother at her North Carolina home. No children or husbands were allowed! Just us girls. Those five days were filled with lengthy conversations, meals when we felt like it, watching such movies as *Enchanted April* (not exactly your action-packed men's film), and shopping.

In the quaint village of Blowing Rock, we spent about an hour in a small accessory shop selecting music tapes. The shop was quiet so the salesperson played tape after tape for us while we decided which ones to buy. We were all singing along with our favorite songs and having a grand time. A woman came in and remarked on how much fun we were having. She said, "Obviously, you're here with women friends and not with your husbands." Her comment caught my attention. "Yes," I replied, "it's just the girls." She looked at us enviously as if she would love to be a part of this cheery, intimate group. "I'm shopping with my husband, and it's not much fun!"

Let's face it, what makes shopping fun for women is the experience of relationships or at least the potential ones that might happen when that right item is found. For most men, shopping is down right boring and pragmatic. "Need shirt, buy shirt, bought shirt." That's it!

Whether in the context of family, marriage, or parenting, in the workplace, in friendships, or within the church, a woman's "identity is defined in a context of relationships and is judged by a standard of responsibility and care."[1] Men seem to be more defined by their vocations and value relationships only as they promote their own goals.

In the past, research on adults was done primarily on men (Freud). Today, thanks to the feminist movement, serious attention has been given to women. Now feminine psychology is in vogue.

## RESEARCH ON FEMALE DIFFERENCES

When the feminist movement caught on in the sixties, the driving impetus was civil rights, equal opportunity, and equal pay. However, whether it was intended or not, the popular expression or interpretation of the movement at the grass roots level was, in my opinion, a belief that there were no essential differences between men and women. Of course, the differences in anatomy were self-evident and acknowledged, but even these were sometimes down played.[2] However, some feminists were serious scholars and researchers.

Today I sense a new direction, being driven by current social, psychological, and biological research. The literature suggests a drastic change from the earlier androgynist view (one human sex) to a more truly feminist or feminine one. Now it seems feminists are encouraging women to be what they already are, rather than striving to be like men. So why has this change come about? The critical research reveals unique differences between the sexes in almost every important area.

## GENDER BRAIN DIFFERENCES

The grand, ongoing debate between "nature and nurture" will probably never be solved to the satisfaction of any real scientist. I find it interesting, from my limited knowledge and lay perspective, that what a person believes about this is very much related to the field he or she works in. Psychologists and sociologists predictably will argue for a greater role on the "nurturing" side. They argue the case for developmental and social influences as the determining factors for one's being and behavior. In other words, little girls are more relational because their society expects them to be. Little boys are raised to be independent and stand on their own two feet.

On the other hand, it seems the physiologists, physicians, neurologists, and geneticists see human behavior as influenced more by biological predispositions. Again, these are giant generalizations based upon very inadequate information.

Anne Moir, a British geneticist, takes the "nature" route when it comes to female/male differences and roots gender differences in the brain. She comments:

> Men are different from women. They are equal only in their common membership of the same species, humankind. To maintain that they are the same in aptitude, skill or behaviour is to build a society based on a biological and scientific lie.
>
> The sexes are different because their brains are different. The brain, the chief administrative and emotional organ of life, is differently constructed in men and in women; it processes information in a different way, which results in different perceptions, priorities and behaviour.
>
> The way our brains are made affects how we think, learn, see, smell, communicate, love, make love, fight, succeed, or fail. Understanding how our brains, and those of others, are made is a matter of no little importance.[3]

What we have learned from these brain studies is that men and women differ radically in the ways their brains are structured and, therefore, in how they function. It has been known for several years that the two sides of the brain have differing functions. The right side controls visual and spatial functions. It perceives the overall picture of life and allows us to understand abstractions, shapes, and patterns. It is also the side of the brain that governs our emotions. In my case, this proves to be a very active part of the brain!

On the left side, we find the verbal, linguistic, and concrete functions. This side of our brain allows us to see and think about details and more practical things in a logical, orderly sequence. An easy way to remember them is that the left side of the brain is the logical side (L for logical); the right side is the relational side (R for relational).

In the past, popular theory stated that men were more left-brain dominant and women more right-brain dominant. However, more recent studies have shown women to have 40 percent more connectors (called the corpus callosum) between the two sides of the brain. Bob says this makes men half-wits. He said it, not me!

## EMOTIONAL DIFFERENCES

What does this difference in brain structure mean for women? One major difference is the emotional makeup due to women's more efficient and integrated exchange of information from one side of the brain to the other. The more connections one has, the more articulate and fluent one is, particularly in expressing what one feels.

### Ability in Expressing Feelings

If more couples were aware of the diversity of their needs and understood why the differences existed, much of the stress and pain would be alleviated. Men and women come to the basic dance of life but bring radically different skills, perceptions, and capabilities. They are often out of step with each other.

Dr. Moir notes,

> A woman brings to the relationship emotional sensitivity, a capacity for interdependence, a yearning for companionship and for sex to reflect that emotional intimacy. A man, if not totally blind to the importance of emotions has a less-demanding emotional nature. He has the capacity for independence, and sees his duties in the marital contract largely in terms of providing financial security. He wants a "good" sex life, as a result of which his wife will "people" the small state of the family he heads . . . and make solid his own foundations in life.[4]

As noted earlier, the wiring of our brains is different. The language women speak and hear is of feeling, nuance, and emotion. The language of men is action, facts, sports, and tools! Women want to share their innermost thoughts, feelings, and fears. They feel connected by simply sharing in the process of this communication. Men feel less comfortable with this form of language. Their brains don't allow them to translate feelings to words as readily as transmitting thoughts into words.

Moir again observes,

> Their capacity to feel is to a greater degree than in women,physically divorced from their capacity to articulate; further,the emotional centres of the male brain are located far morediscretely than in the woman. It's not that he "bottles

things up" . . . more that his emotions are in a separate box, in a separate room, a room not routinely visited.[5]

The difficulty has commonly been explained away by our failure to encourage boys to cry or express pain. I remember when Graham used to play soccer. One afternoon, after his team had played their hearts out and still lost, the little boys were upset and some were crying. I observed one boy walk up to his father, lean his tired little body next to his tall, strong dad, and start to weep quietly. The tears rolled down his cheeks as he looked up into his dad's face for comfort and reassurance. This athletic dad pushed his son away. His next words were, "Don't come crying to me. You guys deserved to lose this game."

Emotions are not viewed in the masculine world as valuable, as a measure of strength or health. Men learn early to do their crying in private. As a matter of fact, many women don't want to see their husbands cry. It scares them. Men cry so seldom that to see them doing so must mean that something terrible has happened. A woman's stability is threatened when she witnesses her husband's vulnerable and needy state. It is a foreign and frightening experience for both. How often did you see your father cry, and how did you feel about it? When was the last time you saw your husband's tears? How did you feel?

Most little girls, on the other hand, cry openly. They cry about everything. It's just part of being a little girl. I don't remember ever being reprimanded for my tears. As little girls progress into the adolescent stage, the hormonal fluctuations cause constant emotional mood swings that continue to plague them until menopause. Men are bewildered and irritated by these mood swings. Dr. Moir writes, "Women cry more often than men perhaps because they have more to cry about—they are receiving more emotional input, reacting more strongly to it and expressing it with greater force."[6]

## Emotional Intuition

Because of this emotional bent, women are more programed to the needs of others, empathize more readily, and carry a great deal of others' emotional baggage. This is their nurturing side in action. Men don't tend to assume the problems of others emotionally. They "do their feeling work" by looking for a viable solution to a problem, solve it, and move on to something else. Because a woman has a larger bundle of fibers connecting both sides of her brain, information is more easily exchanged and she is more in touch with her feelings. Dr. Moir believes this one fact may explain "women's intuition." She writes, "Is the physical capacity of a woman to connect and relate more pieces of information than a man explained, not by witchcraft, after all, but merely by superior switchgear?"[7]

Bob and I were at a party recently. A friend came over and started talking about simple, everyday things. She chatted away, but something just didn't seem right to me. Later I asked Bob if he had noticed anything unusual. He didn't understand what I meant. He said the friend had not mentioned anything wrong, so things must be fine. Later I called this friend. I gently asked her how things were going. She opened up about problems she was having with her husband, confusion about her teenagers, and overall frustrations she was feeling about life.

We women appear to have a sixth sense about others, and our "intuition" antennae are always picking up the hidden messages that our male counterpart misses.

> Women in general are better at recognizing the emotional nuances in voice, gesture, and facial expression that communicate a whole range of sensory information. They can deduce more from such information because they have a greater capacity than men to integrate and cross-relate verbal and visual information.[8]

The male is at a great disadvantage. If emotions are accessed on the right side of the brain, with verbal functions on the left, men have less ability in putting their feelings into words.

## Need for Emotional Support
Through the course of raising three children, Bob and I have had many conversations about different situations and concerns regarding our kids. I usually want to discuss the issue over and over again, expressing and processing my feelings. Bob finally reaches a point where he gets frustrated and wants to cut off discussion unless we can talk about solutions. His response is usually, "Well, what do you want *me* to do about it?" That always drives me crazy! My answer is usually a frustrated, "I don't know!" I'm not necessarily looking for an answer, just a response of mutual concern. At that point I walk away, angry because he doesn't appear to share my feelings. Then I feel totally responsible for the problem and resentful that he won't share in the burden.

The raging gap between men and women in the area of emotional expression can leave women feeling very alone. For the relational woman, an event is often important only because it provides connection with another person. A man may not even want to connect emotionally. He may not feel comfortable with emotions or want to be burdened with the confusing and fear-producing emotions a woman expresses. Therefore, in reality, a great deal of our emotional support will inevitably come from other women who share common interests and relational needs. The bonds of homemaking, motherhood, careers, shopping, and mutual troubles are natural for women—although they drive men crazy. Whether the emotions are joy or sorrow, it is difficult for most men to come alongside in the way another woman can. Nor should we expect them to. I must give men, including Bob, some credit. I think many times they do make sincere efforts to listen, care, and be involved, but we may not recognize it or appreciate it because it wasn't done in a "woman's way."

## Perception of Emotional Intimacy

Carol Gilligan's book *In a Different Voice* has become standard reading in most women's studies programs at the university level. A professor of education at Harvard University, she represents the new wave of educated women constructing and articulating theories of human development based on fair and accurate research. Her primary interest has been in studying women's issues as they relate to identity, perception, and moral dilemmas. She has discovered that "At a time when efforts are being made to eradicate discrimination between the sexes in the search for social equality and justice, the differences between the sexes are being rediscovered in the social sciences."[9]

Dr. Gilligan has also revealed some striking observations about how we as women perceive "intimacy." She conducted a study of images of violence as revealed through the use of the TAT (Thematic Apperception Test). College students were asked to write stories based upon a series of ambiguous pictures. These pictures were of people either sitting in close proximity to one another or maintaining some physical distance. The scenarios were to be based on the students' perception of what was occurring between the people in the pictures. These tests were designed to study male and female responses in the area of affiliation (relationship to one another) and achievement (how one responds to success).

Gilligan concluded:

Men and women may perceive danger in different social situations and construe danger in different ways—men seeing danger more often in close personal affiliation than in achievement and construing danger to arise from intimacy, women perceiving danger in impersonal achievement situations and construing danger to result from competitive success. The danger men describe in their stories of intimacy is a danger of entrapment or betrayal, being caught in a smothering relationship or humiliated by rejection and deceit. In contrast, the danger women portray in their tales of achievement is a danger of isolation, a fear that in standing out or being set apart by success, they will be left alone.[10]

One can conclude that men and women view "closeness" differently. Men must maintain a certain distance to feel close, whereas women must "be close." The opposite is also true. Gilligan notes, "As people are brought closer together in the pictures, the images of violence in the men's stories increases. The women projected violence most frequently when people were further apart." For men, danger exists in close connection, for women in separation and abandonment.[11]

Therefore, a woman travels down a very unique emotional path on her feminine journey. She also finds her emotional life overlaps into the area of communication. Not only how our feelings work differs from men but also how we communicate.

## COMMUNICATION STYLE

Probably one of the most frustrating areas for women as they try to understand and talk to men is communication. At times one would almost think the two genders speak different languages. Enter a professor of linguistics at the prestigious Georgetown University, Deborah Tannen, Ph.D. A self-professed feminist, she has been studying the language styles of men and women for years. Her conclusion? Guess what? Men and women speak and hear different languages! She writes:

I am joining the growing dialogue on gender and language because the risk of ignoring differences is greater than the danger of naming them. Sweeping something big under the rug doesn't make it go away; it trips you up and sends you sprawling when you venture across the room. Denying real differences can only compound the confusion that is already widespread in this era and re-forming relationships between women and men.

The desire to affirm that women are equal has made some scholars reluctant to show they are different, because differences can be used to justify unequal treatment and opportunity. Much as I understand and am in sympathy with those who wish there were no differences between men and women—only reparable social injustice—my research, others' research, and my own and others' experience tell me it simply isn't so. There *are* gender differences in ways of speaking, and we need to identify and understand them. Without such understanding, we are doomed to blame others or ourselves—or the relationship—for the otherwise mystifying and damaging effects of our contrasting conversational styles.[12]

Tannen's work has been on the *New York Times* best-seller list for over ten months, so she must be striking a responsive chord. From her research on language patterns, she concludes that women approach life and the world as individuals living in a network of relationships. Conversations are thus negotiations in an attempt to create or maintain closeness. What a woman is looking for in the negotiation process is confirmation and support for her thinking and feeling.[13]

Men, however, view the world as a hierarchy where communication is more a "jockeying for status" and power, whereby constant "one-upmanship" is the course.[14] In summary, women use language to either gain or maintain relationships, whereas men see language as the means of gaining power and either gathering or dispensing information. Men don't talk unless they have to or need something! In short, we speak and hear different languages. These differences play out in a variety of daily occurrences that can wreak havoc in our relationships.

One evening Bob and I were driving home after going to the movies. It was still early so I suggested, "Would you like to stop and get something to eat?"

Bob replied, "No, I don't think so. I'm not hungry."

I pressed, "Are you sure you don't want to stop?"

Again Bob answered, "No, I'm tired and I want to get home to watch the news before bed."

I felt surprisingly disappointed, leaned back in the car seat, became very quiet, and just stared out the window. We pulled into the garage and as Bob turned off the ignition he looked at me and sensed that all was not well. He asked, "What's wrong?"

My answer: "Oh, nothing."

In typical male fashion he accepted my answer, went inside, turned on the news—and that was that. I went off to get ready for bed and felt very hurt. Later Bob came up and was oblivious to my sullen attitude as he got ready for bed. I sulked around the room, waited for a response that I didn't get, and decided to pursue the issue. "I really wanted to stop off for a bite to eat before coming home. It wasn't that I was terribly hungry, but I thought it would be fun to have a little more time together as long as we were out."

Bob angrily blurted out, "Then why didn't you say so?"

What had happened in this simple exchange? As a woman, I was speaking and hearing a different language than my husband was. As a result of the dialogue, Bob and I had reached vastly different conclusions. I was convinced that Bob cared more about watching the evening news than about spending time with me. Bob was convinced that I, as a woman, never say what I want and even worse, expected him to be able to read my mind.

In reality, what I was trying to do with my first question—"Would you like to stop and get something to eat?"—was to make a connection. In my head, what I was really saying was, "Wouldn't it be fun to just spend a little more time together before we have to go home to the dishes in the sink, the phone calls, and getting kids to bed." What Bob heard was a mere request for information—"Was he hungry?" His response was a blunt, informational "No!"

A woman thinks, speaks, and hears relationally. Her style of communication is built around her network of relationships. A man's is not. Other research would suggest that when women speak they are essentially saying, "Listen to me so you can share and validate my feelings." What the man usually hears in this is a plea to fix something or locate the cause for the feeling.[15] In both instances, the woman rarely receives what she is looking for and comes away from the interaction feeling disappointed and alone.

Some have tried to root these communication differences in the way girls and boys are socialized. However, more and more researchers are discovering that the communication differences are also related to the way our brains operate, originating from birth. We as women speak differently because our brains are wired differently.

Neurologist Richard Restak concludes, "On the basis of the information already available, it seems unrealistic to deny any longer the existence of male and female brain differences. Just as there are physical dissimilarities between males and females (size, body shape, skeleton, teeth, age of puberty, etc.) there are equally dramatic differences in brain functioning."[16]

But can't these differences still be the result of certain social conditioning? Donovan and Wonder, a researcher and a communications consultant, say the differences begin at birth: "At birth there are basic differences between male and female brains. The female cortex is more fully developed. The sound of the human voice elicits more left-brain activity in infant girls than in infant boys, accounting in part for the earlier development in females' language. Baby girls have larger connectors between the brain's hemispheres and thus integrate information more skillfully. This flexibility bestows greater verbal and intuitive skills. We've all seen the little girls at nursery school who just chatter away with each other, using expression, big words, and full sentences. Male infants lack this ready communication between the brain's lobes: Therefore, messages are routed and rerouted to the right brain, producing larger right hemispheres. In the same nursery school, the little boys are playing by themselves making noises like trucks and airplanes with little verbal exchange between other boys, except to fight over a toy. I don't mean to overgeneralize, but you get the point. Researcher Diane McGuiness forms an acceptable premise: "Women and men are different from the very beginning; what needs to be made equal is the value placed upon these differences."[17]

What all this data means is that women have their brains organized and structured to facilitate relationships. Even the two sides of our brains have a "closer" relationship than men's do. This closeness allows us to look at life through a relational lens and be more relationally focused. In the final analysis, if our brains function this way (and the research seems to confirm this), this unique feminine intellectual approach affects how we view the entire world. Our brains influence our entire perception.

Our differing approaches encompass not only what happens in the classroom, but also the bedroom. The sexual aspect of the feminine journey begins in a woman's head long before becoming a physical reality. One of the profound influences upon a woman's mind is the world of make-believe.

## FEMALE FANTASY

Not much has been written on female fantasy. However one illuminating writer has disclosed: "A woman's view of sexuality and romance is a product of the great American fantasy machine."[18] She goes on to write that through a woman's life journey, "The majority of female Americans of today's generation reached adulthood with quite a bit of emotional baggage—two oversized suitcases, a garment bag and assorted hand-held carryons filled with an entourage of imaginary lovers."[19]

God's gift of human imagination has been bombarded and deceived by the secular world of television, movies, romance novels, advertizing, and love songs. Women are brainwashed daily with the message that the entire goal of life is to be involved in passionate pursuit, emotional turmoil, and final sexual conquest. Warren Farrell, acclaimed author and professor at the School of Medicine (University of California, San Diego), points out that 40 percent of all paperback books sold are romance novels, which are purchased predominately, if not exclusively, by women.[20] This is bound to influence a woman's thought life about romance. Meanwhile, men are reading action-packed stories such as *The Firm, Hunt for Red October*, or Louis L'Amore novels. Reading material makes a statement about the values of and differences between the sexes.

It is impossible for any man to live up to the illusive image of the romantic knight in shining armor who delivers the maiden from peril, keeping her totally satisfied in every area throughout her life. The more women read books of this type, the higher their expectations and extensive their romantic fantasies. Thus, they are more disposed to the inevitability of disappointment and frustration with their real "flesh and blood man." Women must not allow their fantasy images of non-reality to rob them of fulfillment and satisfaction in the real world. In one sense, romance novels are a uniquely female form of pornography, but their inherent evil lies in the power to deceive and disappoint.

Are these make-believe male images really what a woman needs and/or wants as she travels along the realities of her journey? Contrary to what the world of entertainment and advertising would like to portray, women have not completely bought into the fantasy world. Farrell's study of the fantasies of over 106,000 men and women show women are still very much in touch with their basic needs even after several decades of contrary socialization. He writes, "a woman's primary fantasy was still security and family."[21] Men have different fantasies.[22]

Despite all the press about the "new woman" for the nineties, it would seem that women's fantasies and values are still very much locked into the old-fashioned hearth-and-home values of the supposedly bygone days.

I don't read things like *The World Almanac*, but for some strange reason God gave me a husband who does. The current listing of best-selling magazines at least demonstrates what women buy when they go to the grocery stores, newsstands, and drugstores. What are the themes illustrated in these top-selling magazines? Is it how to get ahead in your career, invest your income, or plan a leveraged buy-out? No, the themes are the old standard themes of family and home. Look at the list! Six of the ten best-sellers in 1992 were: *Better Homes and Gardens* (8 million), *Family Circle* (5.4 million), *Good Housekeeping* (5.1 million), *McCall's* (5 million), *Ladies Home Journal* (5 million), and *Woman's Day* (4.8 million). *Time* was number eleven at 4 million. By comparison, *New Woman* was number fifty-three with 1.3 million circulation. *Ms.* and *Working Woman* didn't even make the top one hundred. Even *Cooking Light* beat them at number eighty![23]

What does this mean? I believe it means that even though many women today are working and pursuing their careers, and are very educated, deep within their souls is another voice. It is the relational voice that springs forth when they want reading material. Even though they may have other interests and vocations, their ultimate fantasy is that of the home, its furnishings, and the relationships cultivated there. Because of the holistic aspect of her nature, a woman brings not only her fantasies but her whole being into the bedroom. Her relational nature as expressed in her brain, her emotions, and her communication style combines with her fantasies to find full expression as a sexual being. The relational woman is a sexual woman. But even then, her approach and perception about sexuality differs radically from men.

## RELATIONAL SEXUALITY

I was amused by a cartoon that portrayed two men talking to each other while watching a football game. They were laughing and making sexual comments about the cheerleaders. In the kitchen, one of the wives says to the other wife, "Do you think eating cake is better than sex?" The other woman responds, "What kind of cake?"

For some reason, this cartoon made me laugh. It was obviously created by a woman. I don't believe it strikes a humorous chord within us because we don't like sex, but because our view of sex is so altogether different from our husbands'. Bob compares these differences to file folders and waves. Men have a file-folder approach to sexuality. They can move from work to play to sex and on to paying bills, as if they were merely pulling out different files from a cabinet. Women, on the other hand, view the sexual life in a more romantic, oceanic, holistic way. Certain moods must be created throughout the day which, as waves moving toward shore, finally burst on the sandy beaches. The wave starts far away from shore and grows through time. Women flow, men file!

The Christian community has come a long way in acknowledging the need for honest and open teaching concerning the sexual relationship within a marriage.

> People are uneasy with the correlation of sexuality and religion. Christianity, especially, has separated the two in a way that would make them appear to be irreconcilable. The church elevates religion, devaluing sexuality. The union of sexuality and religion is like an electrical connection. Wrong joining leads to disaster. No joining produces no energy. Proper joining holds promise.[24]

The bookshelves contain some excellent literature on the sexual relationship between men and women. The research is fascinating, particularly for women who just don't understand men or who feel confused about their own sexuality.

Whereas the Christian community has ignored the topic of sexuality, the feminist movement has exacerbated it. The feminist message of the exploitation and victimization of women has fanned the flames of anger, hostility, and alienation between the sexes. A certain irony is present in that while sexual liberation was at its height, sexual satisfaction appeared to be ebbing. However, most would agree that men and women differ greatly in their approach to their sexual life.

Psychologist Willard Harley states, "For women, having sex is a decision, more mental than physical."[25] It is approached within the framework of the events of her day, how she feels about herself and a sense of affection and desirability she feels for her husband. These perceptions set the stage that will result in a fulfilling sexual experience for the woman. For men, it is not as complex, or at least, as multidimensional. Harley notes, "To the typical man, sex is like air or water. He doesn't have any 'options.' If a woman fails to understand the power of the male sex appetite, she will wind up with a husband who is tense and frustrated."[26] These mental differences about sexuality are perhaps rooted in something much deeper in both sexes.

## GENDER SEXUAL DIFFERENCES

Throughout a woman's sexual journey, enjoyment mixed with boredom will be found. This confusion is due to the chasm between the sexual desires of men and women. George Gilder in *Men and Marriage* presents an interesting perspective on this issue. His premise is that this difference is due to the differing impact of the sexual experience upon the male and female sense of identity. He writes,

> A woman is not so exclusively dependent on copulation for sexual identity. For her, intercourse is only one of the many sex acts or experiences. Her breasts and her womb symbolize a sex role that extends, at least as a potentiality through pregnancy, childbirth, lactation, suckling and long-term nurture. Rather than a brief performance, female sexuality is a long, unfolding process.[27]

In contrast, according to Gilder, "Manhood, at the most basic level, can be validated and expressed only in action." He writes, "Men must perform" whether it be through sex or their work. This "action role" that men are required to play in our society combined with their hormonal drive creates the infamous male sex drive. Sex becomes of paramount importance to the man while it is a more moderate priority to most women.

If communication or emotional problems exist in a marriage, it will often be revealed in a lack of sexual desire and fulfillment for the woman, more so than for the man. The relational aspect of a woman makes it difficult for her to separate problems in other areas of her life from her sex life. A man is more inclined to compartmentalize his life and able to ignore the problems when he "pulls the sex file out" and engages in the physical satisfaction of the sexual act. Penner writes, "Women tend to shut down when they are unfulfilled sexually and men tend to feel more sexual hunger with lack of fulfillment."[28]

Women need to recognize the power we hold in the sexual area and not use it as a weapon, punishment, or source of manipulation over our husbands.

Our differing feelings about this important area of life also have substantial documentation. The famous Masters and Johnson research (over eleven years of research) divided the human sexual response cycle into four phases: the excitement phase, the plateau phase, the orgasmic phase, and the resolution phase. They concluded that women's sexual response in orgasm is an intricate mixture of psychological, physiological, and social influences.[29] When the female sexual response is compared to that of men, though the phases are the same, the rate at which the different phases are entered and exited differ. Generally, men have a significant "refractory period," a period of time following orgasm when they cannot be sexually stimulated. Women, on the other hand, have no such period of time. Women generally are capable of having multiple orgasms, while this is more difficult for men. For the male, orgasms are genitally centered. For women, the experience is more all-encompassing and is felt through the entire body. A woman is more fully connected to the experience both within herself and her man.[30]

The relational aspects of a woman's sexuality is what defines her uniqueness. Her relational nature is revealed through the experiences of her sexual response. In a study done on women about men, Zilbergeld and Stanton asked women what they wanted from men in the sexual area. The overwhelming response was "a greater sharing of themselves."[31] This confirms what the Hite report also concluded, that "an overwhelming number of women chose affection, intimacy, and love, not orgasm, as their primary enjoyment during intercourse."[32]

The evidence again seems conclusive. Women are not looking for high-impact explosions in sex. We are looking for affection, closeness, and expressions of our felt intimacy. All these traits grow out of our unique relational nature. We are looking for a relationship. Perhaps, this relational drive *is* something much deeper than mere socialization. It is rooted in such things as biology and how we view four walls.

## GENDER DIFFERENCES IN BASIC BIOLOGY

It always amazes me that Bob and I can both go on a diet at the same time and he will drop ten pounds while I have problems losing any.

Some of this is basic biology. As women, we just carry more fat (23 percent more), and have a more difficult time burning it off than men do. Some have alluded to the "nurturing" or relational aspect that allows women to have more stored body fat and energy available for "nurturing" children.[33]

Women also have better color perception—Bob regularly wears a black sock and a blue sock and never notices the difference—and oxygen supply to their brains. At age sixty, women will still have 90 percent of the strength and flexibility that they had at age twenty. Men, on the other hand, will have only about 60 percent. In short, men age faster and run out of energy and strength more quickly than women do.

These differences don't necessarily argue for aspects about the relational women, but they do illustrate the vast differences in even the biological capabilities of men and women. But differences for what? Shopping, of course!

The greater fat percentage explains why we can "shop till we drop" while our husbands are looking for a place to sit down! Speaking of energy, the differing ways we utilize energy also has a profound relation to our own ego orientation.

## FEMALE EGO ORIENTATION

When Bob started his current job, he always came home a little disappointed and down. He couldn't put his finger on why until many weeks had passed. Finally, he explained, "I love the teaching at this school, but I think the reason I come home sort of 'down' is because I really don't have an office." It wasn't a real big deal for him, but it was one of those things that was just nibbling away at him.

There is some evidence suggesting men and women view space (four walls) and their relation to it differently. What these findings reveal is that men enjoy the "safety" of being confined in a context that is their "spot." In other words, a man's ego orientation begins with himself in a safe environment and then moves outward. To move outward in both the spatial and emotional sense costs him significant amounts of energy.[34] After expending himself outside this environment, he must come back to his "spot" in order to feel reenergized. For Bob, not having an office that was his made him feel there was no place for him to recharge his batteries throughout the day of teaching. Now he has his "spot" and is happier!

Women, on the other hand, do not have their ego orientation centered on some isolated spot but more in the context of outer relationships. As women, we start with the outward social context of relationships and then move toward our own inner space. For us, whether we reach the inward space or not, the spatial or physical movement is energizing and worth the trip.[35]

These differences of ego orientation can be seen very graphically in the way modern office work space is laid out. Traditionally, men had their private, closed-door offices. That was their workplace, their "spot." Periodically, they would emerge out of this space, open their doors, and give work to their assistants, who were usually organized with desks facing each other and without any walls for privacy. Today, men do some of the jobs traditionally done by women. Being confined to that "open" space is a little threatening to some men. Top companies are now providing modular panels and carrels in order to create the concept of private offices without private rooms. At the same time, some women executives have "opened" up the private corner office with a window or by placing their desk in the middle of the key people they work with. This, they believe, facilitates better communication and team-building, and moves beyond the "power" male image.[36] To me, it's simply women being and doing what they do best . . . forming relationships!

Here we see the same relational qualities being expressed in how women work, and how they desire to work. Women are energized by being with people, talking face-to-face with them, and relating with them without having to close the door to recuperate. Men find security within four walls, whereas women experience a world that is limiting and stifling in these boxes called offices. They come alive by being with people. We even process information and make decisions differently than men.

## PROCESSING OF INFORMATION

It's your classic company board or committee meeting. The third quarter reports are just in and it's time to look at projections about the fourth. The boss, usually a male, begins, "Now let's look at each quarter and then decide where we should go in the last quarter." Plain, clear direction from the boss. Everybody has a copy of the reports, so the group proceeds to look at the first quarter report, then the second, which promotes some discussion.

Mary, one of the VPs and the only woman, politely says, "I think I know what we should do in this next quarter."

The men turn and look at her in amazement and puzzlement. Finally, one brave soul speaks for the group, "Mary, how could you have any idea where to go when we haven't looked at all the reports yet?"

Mary at this point feels angered and belittled, believing men never listen to women. The men at the table are a little irritated about her "busting" in and offering solutions before it was time for solution brainstorming on the last quarter. She broke the rules!

What transpired at that meeting illustrates the difference between sequential and asequential thinking.[37] Tanenbaum believes that, generally speaking, men's minds work on the basis of sequential thinking. In other words, $A + B + C = D$. There is a logical sequence in which men's minds process information and draw conclusions. However, women have the ability to process information asequentially. In our minds we can figure $A + B = D$. This makes absolutely no sense to men. How can one get D before one looks at A, B, and C? But remember, women have 40 percent more connections between the right and left lobes of their brains. This allows more asequential functions to take place.

Yes, it is very difficult today to hold to the androgynous view that there are no differences between men and women. An understanding and acceptance of these differences give us a greater appreciation of ourselves as women and of men. Without this recognition and acceptance, we can allow these God-given differences to become obstacles to our relationships. We can try to make men into our images as women, or men can try to force us into being male-type women. Both approaches are bad. There is no "better" and no "lesser" gender, just two genders God made in His own image.

## OTHER FEMININE RELATIONAL DIFFERENCES

Cris Evatt summarizes over 180 works on the subject of male/female differences and derives from them sixty of the most significant differences. I will close this section by briefly noting nineteen of the more unique differences women have that say something about our relational natures.

❖ Women smile more than men, even when told not to smile.[38]

❖ Women use self-ridiculing humor, rather than putting others down as men do.[39]

❖ Women say connection with people is more important than having respect.[40]

❖ Women play sports and games primarily for exercise and companionship, not for competition.[41]

❖ Women talk about people, their problems, responses, and men; men talk about things, events, gadgets, etc.[42]

❖ Women gossip as an escape valve; for men gossip is a game of scoring points.[43]

❖ Women apologize more; men accuse more.[44]

❖ Women boast about accomplishments only to entrusted friends; men to everyone.[45]

❖ Women nag more; men intimidate more.[46]

❖ Women want validation of their feelings; men want validation for being right.[47]

❖ Women are emotionally jealous; men are sexually jealous.[48]

❖ Women believe they can change people; men believe people change themselves.[49]

❖ Women have more intimate friends; 90 percent of men say their wives are their best friends.[50]

❖ Women are more trusting of others.[51]

❖ Women lie to avoid hurting others' feelings; men lie to protect or enhance themselves.[52]

❖ Women lean forward, gather closer, and look more directly at other people than men do.[53]

❖ Women's sex appeal is in their warm, animated movement toward others; men in their cool, solid sense of self.[54]

❖ Women are more concerned about the health of others; men keep their health problems to themselves.[55]

❖ Women take risks when it is for their family, relatives, and friends; men just take more risks period.[56]

A full listing of all sixty differences is found in the appendix of this book. Read this list to learn more about the impact of these differences on a woman's relationships.

How can all this evidence be explained? Or perhaps a better question in light of these differences is how in the world can a women find a relationship with a man satisfying? To answer this question we must look at the biblical record.

## THE RELATIONAL WOMAN: A BIBLICAL PERSPECTIVE

As noted earlier, when God created the man, *'adam*, He fashioned the human species in two kinds, male and female. But when the woman was fashioned from Adam's rib, she was called by the name *'ishshah*, or woman (Genesis 2:23). The source or etymology of this term is uncertain. Like the Hebrew term *'ish*, "man," *'ishshah* may be a primary noun with no real connection to any other Hebrew term.[57] However, it is used in the Old Testament 775 times, and is the primary term for "woman." As such it depicts some major aspects of what a woman's journey is all about.

### A Woman in Differentiation

The term *'ishshah* first of all reflects a woman's differentiation. She is a male but different. Isn't it amazing we have had to wait for the social and physical scientists finally to confirm this long-standing knowledge as true! Differentiation is seen in a woman's childbearing function. Sarah confesses she is beyond the age of "the manner of women" (Genesis 18:11). Even menstruation is called the "way of women," literally "way of *'ishshah*." Rachel offers this as an excuse to her own father when she had stolen the family idols (see Genesis 31:35). What woman hasn't used her menstrual period as an excuse to get out of high school gym class! Differentiation in the Old Testament was even taken to the "extreme" of having different clothing for each gender regulated by the Mosaic Law. Apparently, anything which sought to break down the line between the sexes was to be viewed as "abomination" in Israel (Deuteronomy 22:5). The message was clear then: Clothing was a "conspicuous sign of the divinely created sexual differentiation."[58] Transvestites didn't go over real well in ancient Israel!

This "way of women" is what distinguishes women from men. Men cannot menstruate, give birth, or nurse. However, hidden in each of these unique functions lies the woman's relational aspect. What is the purpose of the monthly feminine cycle? What is the purpose of being able to nurse? Again, these characteristics imply and stand for the feminine-focused otherness that is so unique to women. There indeed is a way about being a woman that differs from the "way of a man." It's interesting that Rachel knew to use this feminine function to cover her own deceit. It's equally telling that her father wanted no more to do with her upon learning of her condition!

## Relationship with People, Things, and God

The primary way *'ishshah* is viewed in the Old Testament is in the relationship with her husband. Here she is seen as a man's fiancée (Deuteronomy 22:24), wife (Genesis 4:19, 1 Samuel 25:43), wife of another man (Deuteronomy 22:22), the wife of one's youth (Proverbs 5:18), a forsaken and abandoned wife (Isaiah 54:6), and a wife of her husband's bosom (Deuteronomy 28:54). She is even relational when found in negative illustrations: a woman of fornication (Joshua 2:1), a wife of harlotry (Hosea 1:2), and a loose or strange woman (Proverbs 2:16; 5:3,20). Even in these passages she is defined by the relationship she has with others, especially men. Lest we think these "negative" relationships find no value or worth in Scripture, we need to be reminded that in the genealogy of our Lord, four women (*'ishshahs*) of less cultural standing are found: Tamar, who had intercourse with her father-in-law; Rahab, the harlot; Ruth, a Moabitess who obtained her husband by lying with him on the threshing floor; and Bathsheba, an adulteress. In addition, Mary, the mother of Jesus, was herself suspected of having intercourse prior to her marriage to Joseph (Matthew 1:18).[59]

Now, I know some single readers may be asking, "But wait, I'm single, how can I continue on this feminine journey if I have no man?" It would seem the usage of both *'ishshah* and its Greek counterpart, *gune*, have a much broader meaning.

*Gune* also represents this relational aspect. One scholar notes, "In general Greek, from the time of Homer, as also in the LXX (Greek translation of the Old Testament) and the NT, gune denotes a. the 'female' as distinct from the male and the wife of another."[60]

All these usages reflect the relational element of the woman's (*'ishshah* and *gune*) journey. She is defined and finds her identity in the context of others, particularly her husband and family. However, as important and primary as this is, her identity is not limited to that of being wife and mother. Even though the Bible is sometimes viewed as encouraging strict roles for men and women, I see a certain openness or normalcy that goes beyond any narrowly defined role. When a person takes the time to read more widely, one finds mention of a "woman of wealth" (2 Kings 4:8, NIV), who initiates building a special (and probably well-decorated) room in her house for the prophet Elisha. She is commended for her "relational" consideration of the prophet, but it is implicit in the text that she is a woman of great importance. This well-to-do woman of Shunem, and her surprisingly unnamed husband, is set in stark contrast to the widow Elisha met earlier. Both are *'ishshahs*—one widowed, the other wealthy—acting relationally and using their material assets, at whatever level, in caring for children and ministry (2 Kings 4:1,9).

Deborah was apparently better known for being a prophetess and judge than as the wife of Lappidoth (Judges 4:4). Her claim to fame is not her marriage, but even perhaps, in spite of it. Deborah is commended for doing what the men should have done at that time— namely, take up arms and fight the Canaanites (Hebrews 11:34).[61] Here again, one could argue that though Deborah was both wife and mother, she was far more than what those relationships defined for her. She became a military general, commanding the entire army of Israel. That would be like a female chairperson of the Joint Chiefs of Staff! Miriam, the sister of Moses, likewise is called a prophetess (Exodus 15:20), along with Huldah, the wife of Shallum (2 Kings 22:14), and Isaiah's wife (Isaiah 8:3).

It would seem that being a relational woman does not mean you must restrict your relational skills and gifts to use in the home. The relational woman must somehow find the balance between her connection to the people she loves and being true to herself as an individual.

Not all women may be called to be married, or to have a family, or to find all their relational needs and wants fulfilled by being relational in a home environment. There have always been the Deborahs and women of wealth who have related better to Christian communities, society's ills, national crisis, or formal institutions than to their own homes. For some women, life may seem "out of sync" and different seasons call for appropriate responses.

Janie was single until the age of thirty-eight. She describes her single years as "alternating waves of contentment and of frustration." She openly admits her relational needs were most satisfied through her married friends. She commented, "With other single women there was always the subtle undercurrent of competition. With couples I felt free to be myself, and particularly safe with those husbands as I didn't feel compelled to perform."

Janie now credits her realistic view of marriage and its adjustments to her single years of observing married couples. She admits that being single was frustrating in her twenties; however, in her thirties, she realized that she was wasting time and energy focusing on the 10 percent of her life that was not being fulfilled. Good advice for all of us!

Some women combine ministry and marriage. Priscilla may be one such woman. As a New Testament woman, she combined her relational skills with her love of God and made a significant impact on the early Christian church. Not a great deal is written about Priscilla and her husband, Aquila. However, as we trace the journey of this woman, in concert with her husband, it becomes clear that she viewed her home and her ministry as one and the same. Her life illustrates that a woman's ministry is not necessarily a task performed outside of marriage or in spite of it, but as a natural outgrowth and extension. We can see Priscilla's commitment in four basic areas.

Priscilla had a commitment to God's Word. For a year and a half, Priscilla and Aquila sat under the teaching of the Apostle Paul (Acts 18:11). Their knowledge of Scripture was such that God used them to correct Apollos, a dynamic young teacher, who apparently lacked in some area of biblical understanding (Acts 18:24-26). At a time when Jewish women were separated from men during religious teaching, we find a woman who was engaging, developing her mind and her spirit.

Priscilla also evidences a commitment to God's work. Everywhere Priscilla and Aquila went, a ministry happened. In Corinth they had invited Paul into their home, where many probably came to be taught and ministered to. Paul then took them to Ephesus, where they laid the groundwork for a church. Later they even had a church meeting in their home (1 Corinthians 16:19). Though their profession was tent-making, their vocation (calling) was church-making. In Priscilla we find a courageous woman who, despite the persecution and turbulence surrounding Paul and his ministry, was not afraid to be connected to God's work.

Priscilla also had a concern for the world. She and Aquila were amazingly mobile. Every time we meet them they are in a different city. They were able to go where they were most needed in the service of the Messiah. Aquila was born in Pontus (Acts 18:2), so it is probable that Priscilla was also a Pontian. However, it is clear that this couple considered themselves pilgrims and ambassadors for Christ rather than citizens of one local community (2 Corinthians 5:20). The more Priscilla saw of the world, the greater her concern that God's truth penetrate the lives of those around her.

Priscilla is certainly a model woman, who contrary to many norms kept pulling up stakes, moving internationally across racial and cultural boundaries, in order to make her life count for more than just how well she kept her own home!

Priscilla, was relational to the core. We can clearly see her commitment to God's workers. On whom did Priscilla and Aquila, a lay couple, have an impact? On some of the greatest names in first-century Christianity: Apollos, Timothy, and Paul. Paul, the author of almost half of the New Testament, was especially close to this couple. He saw in them a woman and a man who illustrated that marriage and ministry do not have to be separate categories. This couple had a team ministry; one that began with the Word, worked through the home in natural ways, invaded the world, and ministered to God's workers along the way.[62]

But can the closeness of marriage or ministry ever be too much closeness? Can a woman with all her relational drives see these desires for closeness become liabilities rather than strengths?

## CONNECTION OR INDEPENDENCE?

Finding a healthy balance in one's identity is never an easy task. There is much written today on the codependency of women and the problems they face in enmeshing too much with their husband's and children's lives. There is also the more recent feminist extreme of individualization, viewing any dependent relationship a woman might have as inherently wrong. I know. I have struggled at both extremes.

It is interesting to watch science discover and confirm how God designed the genders. The critical factor in these findings hinges on the relationship between a child and the mother. Carol Gilligan again gives insight: "For boys and men, separation and individuation are critically tied to gender identity since separation from the mother is essential for the development of masculinity."[63] She continues, "For girls and women, issues of femininity or feminine identity do not depend on the achievement of separation from the other or on the process of individuation."[64] She concludes that the "male gender identity is threatened by intimacy while female gender identity is threatened by separation. Thus, males tend to have difficulty with relationships, while females tend to have problems with individuation."

These issues of separation and individualization are crucial to understand. They surface within marriage and the home, as this is the predominant place where, if women are married, we will look for intimacy and identity. For those not married, the workplace, extended family, and friends may also meet these relational needs and bring challenges.

Often the greatest challenge is to have the ability to maintain and protect healthy boundaries of one's personhood. The feminist movement tells women to "be their own woman." The Christian community admonishes women to give themselves away. Both messages are true in part, but prove harmful when taken to extremes.

It is my contention that women, in general, err on the side of giving too much of themselves away—particularly in the Christian community. Issues of dependence and the need to feel connection create an inclination for women to sacrifice whatever is necessary to maintain relationships and avoid isolation.

Many women feel it is their obligation to take on an exaggerated sense of responsibility for everyone and their problems. This can lead to a controlling, contentious woman who drives her family away and her husband to the housetop or desert rather than to face her contention (Proverbs 21:19, 25:24). Due to her fears, insecurities, or guilt, she may tear her own house apart, brick by brick, as she tries to control, in the guise of care, everyone's life.

Other women find an answer in compliance. Women with backgrounds of neglect, abuse, or lack of nurture may find it easier to please everyone and disregard their own needs and desires. This kind of woman may have never felt the affirmation of her own personhood so she assumes that she has no significant identity or value apart from her connection to others.

In recent times, the term "codependency" has defined the empty and painful lives of many women. Nancy Groom, in *From Bondage to Bonding*, gives a excellent definition:

> Codependency is a self-focused way of life in which a person blind to his or her true self continually reacts to others being controlled by and seeking to control their behavior, attitudes, and/or opinions, resulting in spiritual sterility, loss of authenticity, and absence of intimacy.[65]

Groom also notes, "Codependency holds a person hostage to other people's behaviors, moods, or opinions, and the codependent bases his or her worth and actions on someone else's life. It is a terrible bondage."[66]

The codependent woman is void of clear boundaries. Dr. Henry Cloud and Dr. John Townsend's *Boundaries* reveals the difficulties experienced in a life that is too enmeshed in others:

Boundaries define us. They define what is me and what is not me. A boundary shows me where I end and someone else begins, leading me to a sense of ownership. In addition to showing us what we are responsible for, boundaries help us to define what is not on our property and what we are not responsible for.[67]

One "teaching" that promotes if not facilitates a certain degree of codependency and loss of boundaries is that of submission. Submission has been one of the most misunderstood and often abused responsibilities among Christian women. It is the downside of the spiritually correct, submissive, relational woman. Groom articulates the struggles of submission in her book *Married Without Masks*. She describes the inappropriate methods women have devised, and the masks they wear, within the marriage relationship as they use submission to either avoid personal responsibility for their own lives or to control their husbands. She confronts the battle between "inner" submission and "outward" submission. She writes, "This inner submission, if it is honestly examined, is the point at which the struggle for integrity is waged in the souls of most women."[68] How does a married woman submit to her husband without losing her own identity and value? "The tightrope between personal competence and appropriate dependence in a marriage relationship is not easy for a woman to walk,"[69] says Nancy Groom. I agree. It takes a whole, personally competent person who has a sense of her own boundaries to submit properly to anyone or anything. Submission is a choice among other true choices for the truly relational woman.

Women today bring into the marriage relationship a tremendous amount of baggage from their childhood experiences, unrealistic expectations, erroneous assumptions, negative self-image, and sin nature. Once the "bloom is off the rose," and the romance becomes deluded with personality differences, financial stress, difficulties, and children, the marriage relationship begins to wilt. For many, marriage becomes just another "bag" to bear and discard eventually on life's journey. For others, it becomes the pivotal place to face one's self, take off masks, and become personally responsible while terribly dependent on God's truths.

Many women would rather "go with the flow" in their marriages, dissatisfying as that might be, rather than face the turbulent waters of change. Change is always painful, and many of us don't have the courage to face it. Fear of rejection, loss, and possible verbal, emotional, or even physical abuse keep many Christian women locked in dysfunctional systems. "Fearing—consciously or unconsciously—that their feelings may not be positive, they choose to work hard at polishing up the exterior of their public or family marriage in hopes that the inner discontent will somehow diminish or disappear altogether."[70] Some women would rather live in a prison they know and understand than jump over the wall. This doesn't mean they leave the boundaries of the marriage, but they must leave the bondage of denial, anger, and dishonesty. The truth can hurt. It can hurt our pride, shatter our images and illusions, and be disruptive temporarily. However, Jesus never shied away from the truth. Being Truth Incarnate, He said, "You shall know the truth, and the truth shall make you free" (John 8:32). Today, we have far more truth about ourselves, our marriages, and our differences. In this sense, we are more free to be who God created us to be.

Scripture reveals God's love and grace for us; it shows how we should treat one another; it affirms His declaration that each one of us is forgiven and that we are each a unique expression of Him. If a woman cannot see her feminine self through the "though fallen—yet redeemed eyes of God," then she will never understand nor truly possess who she really is.

My personal journey, as a relational woman gone awry, took me into a cave of anger, hurt, disillusionment, confusion, and blame. I muddled around in the cave for a while and enjoyed the darkness. Gradually, I noticed it is lonely in a dark cave and certainly not very inviting for someone else to join in. I couldn't—or maybe didn't want to—find my way out. Sometimes God just lets us alone, patiently waiting for us to come to the end of our foolishness, embrace our pain, release our anger, and finally call to Him. In time, as I refocused my eyes in the darkness, I saw the light of God's love and grace.

I was reminded again that "The wise woman builds her house; but the foolish tears it down with her own hands" (Proverbs 14:1). The time of tearing down had to stop and a time of forgiveness and restoration began. Too many women, in the process of "finding themselves" have lost too much in the process. There has to be balance. As Jesus aptly put it, "What will a [woman] be profited, if [she] gains the whole world and forfeits [her] soul?" (Matthew 16:26). Can a woman lose her own soul while trying to find it?

A "straw woman" has been created, fashioned in the form of a perfect feminine goddess. She is a super-woman capable of managing relationships, corporations, and home in a single bound. Contemporary women fall down and worship at her shrine. But this goddess is no nurturer; she is a destroyer of unborn children, who wars with men and emasculates the hunting grounds upon which men have historically proven their manhood. All the while, chipping away at the relational inadequacies of the males in her own home.

Sooner, if not later, whether of her own making or of some tragedy thrust upon her, the journey of a woman's life leads her down the path of woundedness. The "dark nights of the soul" experienced along the corridors of woundedness seem like permanent detours, or worse, dead-end streets. But the biblical perspective charts them as the necessary losses that lead a woman to maturity.

CHAPTER SIX

# THE WOUNDED WOMAN: NECESSARY LOSSES

❦

*Time wounds all heels.*
JANE ACE

*The way I see it, if you want the rainbow,*
*You gotta put up with the rain.*
DOLLY PARTON

Sue was an intelligent, attractive wife and mother of four children, all in their teen years. Her husband, Bill, was a larger-than-life kind of guy who left a sense of his presence wherever he went. He had worked hard through the past nineteen years to achieve success in his own business and had provided a comfortable life for the family. Out of nowhere, with no warning, Bill died on the tennis court, playing the game he loved with all the energy and drive that he had approached everything in life. Sue was left with four teenagers to raise, a thriving business that needed attention, and a future that no longer included Bill.

Two years later, Sue's oldest son was accidentally killed. Sue remembers a conversation she had with God some time later. She lay in bed weeping as she looked for all the places the phrase "it is enough" is found in Scripture. She cried out to the Lord, "I will not be hurt anymore. I just can't take any more." It was as if Sue heard an audible voice saying, "You won't have to be hurt anymore. However, if you don't want to be hurt, you cannot love." In spite of her grief and tears Sue immediately responded, "Then hurt me all you want. I cannot live without love."

Sue was the first in her circle of friends to experience the loss of a husband. Loneliness was her greatest struggle, even though her friends diligently included her in their activities. Her one regret, as she looks back over twenty years, was not allowing herself enough time to grieve together with her children.

We all know women whose feminine journeys have been interrupted by the unexpected and devastating detour of woundedness. Eventually, it will happen to us all in one way or another. Woundedness is an experience of loss; it is a recurrent theme that flows in various forms through all of life. Judith Viorst, in her bestselling book, *Necessary Losses*, writes:

> For the road to human development is paved with renunciation. Throughout our life we grow by giving up. We give up some of our deepest attachments to others. We give up certain cherished parts of ourselves. We must confront, in the dreams we dream, as well as in our intimate relationships, all that we never will have and never will be. Passionate investment leaves us vulnerable to loss. And sometimes, no matter how clever we are, we must lose.[1]

Losses in the form of unexpected changes weave themselves into our life's journey. Some of these are easily negotiated, and some seem to detour us forever. They include: being separated by distance from those we love; the conscious and unconscious losses of unmet expectations and dreams; the loss of romance, employment, and job security; violations of personal safety; broken and troubled relationships; and even loss of our youth. All losses are painful as they force uninvited and threatening change into our lives, thrust us out of our comfort zones, and weigh us down with the insecurities of the unknown.

The greatest impact is felt with the loss of a loved one, particularly a spouse or child. Statistics confirm that most married women will outlive their husbands and will have to find their way through the maze of widowhood. Some may have time to anticipate their grief through a long illness, or death may come as a thief in the night to steal your loved one. Regardless, the loss created through death is an invasion and violation, shattering one's plans, one's place in the world, and one's perspective on the meaning of life.

## WIDOWHOOD

Kate Convissor, in her book *Young Widow*, shares how God walked with her when her husband's tragic accident left her alone and pregnant with their fifth child. She writes:

Widows. Suddenly we have joined a select community, one we had never thought to enter. We are sisters of sorrow, daughters of the void. Suddenly our identity is linked to what we have lost: husband, marriage, father of our children, friend, provider. After years of bounty, suddenly we are the empty ones.

How can this be? Why is the steady current of a life that was years in the making so utterly destroyed? Why is tomorrow so hostile and insecure? We absorb the meaning of forever slowly as the days pass like beads on a ring, until we have toted up so many that we begin to understand—he is not coming back.[2]

Death is the most certain fact of life, the one experience no one can escape. Why then does it take most of us by surprise? Why does it usually find us so unprepared? As I began to write this chapter, I found myself at a loss. Even though I have had to deal with other kinds of losses, widowhood is one experience I have yet to journey through. Therefore, I found it difficult to bring insight and sensitivity to this subject, and to the depth of pain and loss that it represents.

I have, therefore, read about the experiences of others and talked to those who have made this painful journey in order to shed light on and better understand this stage of a woman's life. I was surprised by the dearth of information written on the subject of widowhood. It is as if society, on the whole, has ignored it, minimizing or dismissing the impact of an event that, in truth, shakes the very foundation of our existence.

Lynn Caine was a woman I discovered who articulated well the confusion and plight of the widow. Faced with her husband's cancer and ultimate death, she found herself in a state of denial and unpreparedness. She wrote, "In my impeccable ignorance of death and dying, I did everything wrong."[3]

Caine's mistakes and struggles prompted her to write a best-selling autobiography entitled *Widow*. In the book she writes very frankly about the high cost of her ignorance and the unnecessary pain caused by her unfamiliarity with the impact of death. She details the irrationality of her behavior as she sought to make sense of her situation. (When she didn't know what to do with her wedding ring, in her painful confusion, she threw it out of her car window!)

Her second book, *Being a Widow*, deals more realistically and effectively with the problems that accompany the grief of being a widow. The overriding truth about widowhood is that it creates a unique sense of grievous loss due to a sense of powerlessness and displacement. Caine writes,

> It is the widow who is experiencing the loss, who is grieving, who cannot erase the source of her pain. She cannot delete it from her life. That makes her different from you, and makes her feel less in charge of her own fate. She is set apart from other people because her husband is dead. It makes her angry, resentful. Other women have husbands. She doesn't. Your life goes on, but she feels that the future has been grabbed right out of her hands. That makes her extremely sensitive to the things you say or do. The widow cannot tell people how to act toward her because for the most part, they don't listen.[4]

Therefore, it is important that we understand the widow's experiences, feelings, and needs in order to help others as well as to prepare ourselves for this stage of our feminine journey. It will be a reality for the majority of us. For most, widowhood will be a tragic loss, while for a few, it may bring with it a sense of relief and freedom. Regardless, the impact of death will not leave us untouched nor unchanged.

## THE LOSSES OF WIDOWHOOD

When a woman loses her spouse, she loses more than her husband. She loses her old, familiar world as she knows it and in particular, her place and identity in that world.

> After my husband died, I felt like one of those spiraled shells washed up on the beach. Poke a straw through the twisting tunnel, around and around, and there is nothing there. No flesh. No life. Whatever lived there is dried up and gone.
>
> Our society is set up so that most women lose their identities when their husbands die. Marriage is a symbiotic relationship for most of us. We draw our identities from our husbands. We add ourselves to our men, pour ourselves into them and their lives. We exist in their reflection. And then . . . ? If they die . . . ? What is left? It's wrenching enough to lose the man who is your lover, your companion, your best friend, the father of your children, without losing yourself as well.[5]

In a world that places great value on being a "couple," the loss of this couple identification is what pulls the rug out from under the widow. It shakes the very foundation of a life that has been built on the concept of "two" and is now reduced to a foundation of "one."

Xenia Rose, wife of famous cellist Leonard Rose, struggled greatly with this sense of lost identification. Married to a world-famous musician and teacher, she had learned to walk in the shadow of his fame through twenty years of marriage. She writes in her book, *Widow's Journey:*

> This couple identity was much more than an attachment; it became a source of self-identification and self-worth. We became each other's mirrors. Our identities were being redefined by our mutual roles, by our increasingly gratifying interactions and above all, by the reinforcement of our competence.
>
> We reassured, validated, reinforced, and encouraged. We mirrored the best of each other. I lost that mirror when Leonard died. It was a double death. When he had said, "You're wonderful," I believed him because of the interaction between us. At other times he had been critical, and was right to be so, and I managed to change because of him. Now I wasn't so sure.
>
> But with Leonard gone, I felt paralyzed. It was as if he had taken a major part of me with him. I also felt the loss of a mirror in very concrete ways. I had always been able to dress in five minutes, but now I was anxious and unsure. I would gaze at myself, trying to decided what to wear, my room littered with rejected clothes.[6]

For many women, this loss of identity is projected through feelings of abandonment, aloneness, and inadequacy. These feelings either whisper or scream at the widow in an inner language of loss every minute of every day and night. It's a language that communicates guilt, fear, anger, and misery as the widow is beginning to process the natural stages of grief. Life is now filled with periods of time where one is either totally consumed with emotions or totally void of emotions.

One may bounce back and forth like a yo-yo pulled by the string of daily reminders. These daily reminders of the absence of your other half are different for each woman. One may be getting the car serviced when that was once your husband's responsibility. For many, there are the endless piles of insurance papers to fill out, the paper trail created by a husband's long-term illness. For some, the overwhelming heap of unpaid bills or the need to balance the checkbook throws them into a panic. Feelings of betrayal and anger explode at the deceased spouse; how could he have died and left her with such burdens when these were his responsibilities? Suddenly the credit cards may be cancelled, if they were in the husband's name, and the woman feels robbed.

Who are you now? Do you still wear your wedding ring, are you still married, or are you now single? What do you call yourself? Xenia Rose describes her frustration and indecision at having to order new stationery. She writes,

> It might sound trivial, but what do you call yourself? Are you still Mrs. So-and-So, your husband's name, or Mrs. Your Name? Or just plain Your Name and no Mrs.?
>
> I recall trying to order stationery a few months after Leonard died, feeling as if the decision, once made, would tell me who I was. All I'd have to do was open my stationery box and there I'd be.[7]

In addition to the loss of one's identity is the loss of being especially loved. My stepfather had a knack for buying Mother unique and meaningful gifts that only he knew she wanted or needed. My mother told me one day, "What is so painful about being alone is that there is no one who loves you best." Gone are the feelings of knowing you are special. Although you may have children and friends, there is that painful awareness that you are no longer first in anyone's life.

Hand in hand with this loss is the acute awareness that the primary recipient of your care and nurturing is gone. Now there is no one to take care of but yourself. Again, there may be friends and children who need you occasionally, but *you* are now your sole responsibility.

Taking care of yourself may be the most difficult area to attend to. For the woman who was so used to caring for her husband, it is a new twist to think about herself first. Meals become a dreaded event, highlighting one's aloneness. It's no fun to cook for one and eat in solitude. The woman may find herself not eating properly or standing at the kitchen sink eating out of a can. Her thoughts are, *Why make the effort? Who really cares?* You need to care about you. A widow may not want to take care of herself, but as she assumes the responsibility she will find a new sense of confidence and growth.

For the many women who journey through the dark waters of widowhood with God as their companion, their language of loss seems to be laced with the comfort of God's love and sustaining grace. My observations, as I read both Christian and secular stories about widowhood, was the sense of aloneness for the women without God and the sense of divine comfort and presence for those with Him. How difficult to face such an upheaval in one's life and feel that it must be endured, managed, and understood solely through human understanding, human strength, and personal stoicism.

I do not mean to say that the death of a spouse is any easier for women with faith than for those without it. For many, there is tremendous anger at God as they proceed through the blaming stage of grief. Faith is a very personal issue that can give some an immediate sense of God's presence and power. For others, their faith will dissolve and cause them to reject God.

> Crisis leans heavily on our assumptions about life. Some of our ideas may shatter, others are strained or readjusted and others stand firm. With the loss of our husband, what we thought was true and dependable—our marriage, our beliefs about death and God, the safety of our world and health of our bodies—has begun to heave and quake. What can we count on![8]

Faith does not necessarily answer all the questions about the tragic event. What it does do is free the mourner from the need to find the meaning of it; it provides an answer for the question why. All will ask that question, but many will move on to the who—the one from whom they are seeking meaning. God is the who. Kate Convissor explains: "Faith also delivers us from the temptation to believe that events are random and inchoate, that life is meaningless. Faith doesn't provide answers; it stands silently—pointing. It whispers rather than shouts, draws instead of pushing."[9] We can be assured that God cares about our loss. In the words of the psalmist,

> Precious in the sight of the LORD
> Is the death of His godly ones. (Psalm 116:15)

The loss felt by the widow is shared by those who have suffered other kinds of losses. Research over the past decade has learned much about these loss reactions. In this sense, the widow's experience becomes a metaphor for the experience of all wounded women. Even Scripture presents the widow as a representative of all who have been abandoned, violated, and innocently wounded by life events.

Therefore, it is informative and encouraging to observe Scripture's consideration of the widow and how biblical writers have enlisted the community and the church to care for them.

## A BIBLICAL PORTRAIT OF WOUNDEDNESS: THE WIDOW

In Scripture, we find that the experience of woundedness is a normative stage in a woman's life. Our God has not deceived us into thinking that life in this world will be free of loss or pain. In fact, the loss of life, property, health, and family are experiences that biblical characters routinely faced. It is only in these modern times that we have grown accustomed to the expectations of good health, long life, well-adjusted children, and secure employment. When these expectations are not fulfilled we cry out to God, either blaming Him or denying Him, for not meeting His "promises" to us. One serious read of the Bible confronts the unrealistic expectations we have about life.

The Scriptures clearly reveal that women are maliciously used sexually (Genesis 38:1-30); that their husbands die leaving them destitute (Ruth); that they suffer the loss of children (1 Kings 17:17-24; Job 1:2,18-19; Luke 7:12); that their leaders oppress them and take their precious property away (Ezekiel 22:7,25); and that they are robbed (Mark 12:40) and neglected (Acts 6:1). The Bible does not airbrush away this stage of woundedness. One cannot read the pages of Scripture without recognizing this common experience.

In the terminology of both testaments, the "widow" becomes the symbol for all who are needy, helpless, and suffering loss.[10] The Hebrew term 'almanah, usually translated "widow," is derived from the verb 'alam, which means "one bound in pain, or unable to speak." Another related noun, 'elem, takes on the meaning of "silence."[11] These meanings provide a graphic picture of the experience of woundedness. Under the name of "widow," the experience is described of a woman being so wrapped up or bound in her pain that she is reduced to speechlessness. She has been silenced and slain by the arrows of outrageous misfortune. The loss of an important relationship closes her mouth in pain.

The New Testament word for widow (chera) also picks up this

idea of neediness and adds the related ideas of being abandoned, renounced, and reduced to living in solitude.[12] One commentator connects the word for widow with another Greek term, *choros*, and suggests the related idea of "empty space," which may also add some understanding to the term.[13] Interestingly, some women I interviewed for this chapter used the word *empty* when commenting about their widowhood experience. Apparently, women haven't changed. The biblical experience is our experience as women. Widowhood, encompassing all women who suffer woundedness, is a condition women face as a part of their feminine journey. This being the case, it is essential to see what other insights we can find about the widow in Scripture.

**Wounded by Life but Not Abandoned by God**
When Naomi married, she was probably like all other Jewish girls, with high hopes and thoughts of marriage, children, and eventually grandchildren. But when she returned to her hometown from the plains of Moab, a widow and childless after the loss of both her sons, her life seemed to run head-on with a cruel fate. She told her fellow townspeople to no longer call her Naomi, Hebrew for "pleasant," but Mara, Hebrew for "bitter." She explained this name change:

> "Do not call me Naomi; call me Mara, for the Almighty has dealt very bitterly with me. I went out full, but the LORD has brought me back empty. Why do you call me Naomi, since the LORD has witnessed against me and the Almighty has afflicted me?"
> (Ruth 1:20-21)

These are the honest feelings and expressions of a wounded woman. They are uttered by one who lost all her important relationships and had to deal with the resultant bitterness. Her emotions are properly placed. In her pain she acknowledges the sovereign God who stands behind the historical scene directing the human tragedy. Even her bitterness is, in reality, her cry of faith. As she embraces her pain and blame, she recognizes the purposes of God, even though she does not like them. At this point, it is easy for many women to jump ship and throw God, the church, and their personal faith to the wind.

I know one young mother who never prayed conversationally during our women's prayer time. When I asked her about it, she confessed, "I guess I haven't really been able to pray since my two-year-old daughter was tragically killed." In an almost unconscious way she had taken the position that because God had taken her only daughter, she would no longer talk to the One who did such a thing. The loss of her daughter had made her bitter. She was a wounded woman still in the process of working through this difficult stage of her journey.

Her conclusion about the working of God in tragedy, I believe, is a natural human reaction. We think God is either the active agent behind our suffering and pain, or He has totally vacated the premises of the universe. This wrestling with God only adds to our pain. Bob has often observed that believers handle difficulty worse than nonbelievers. People who don't know or care anything about God simply have to deal with the tragedy. Believers, on the other hand, have to work through the tragedy and then wrestle with God about it also! However, the full biblical picture about God's involvement in the life of the widow and all other innocent victims is not complete without a broader recognition.

Because as women it is difficult for us to separate our feelings from our thoughts, our thinking about God is sometimes only a reaction to our feelings. Because we feel abandoned by the Deity, we believe we have been.

However, one of the major themes about the widow in Scripture is the reality that God draws especially near to the innocent (alien), the helpless (widow), and the orphan. The widow is always mentioned in these lists, along with the assurance that God, in particular, defends and comes to the aid of the wounded (Exodus 22:22; Deuteronomy 10:18; Psalm 68:5-6, 146:9). Apparently, God sovereignly protects the real estate of widows (Proverbs 15:25), and promises to come against those who oppress them (Malachi 3:5). In other words, when a woman faces the wounds of life, God does not withdrawn His presence from her. In fact, the reverse may be true: He has drawn especially close to her, but in her wounded state she cannot see His presence. As one writer said, "It is hard to see clearly with tears in your eyes." Perhaps at this stage of the journey one has to grasp the "tough faith" concept of entrusting to God our feelings about His absence. We must acknowledge the reality that God can be very present in our feelings of His absence.

This was Job's experience, Naomi's experience, and our Lord's experience on the cross. In His human condition, Jesus cried out, "My God, My God, why hast Thou forsaken Me?" (Mark 15:34). The feeling of being forsaken was real, human emotion. But in reality, God was there—on the cross, behind it, in front of it, above it, and underneath it. God had not fled the historical scene at all; He was still carefully orchestrating the redemptive moment.

Until we can picture God as being in our feelings of His absence or in our worst pains, we haven't embraced what it really means to believe in a God who is omnipresent and immanent at the same time. Our God is really present at all times, in everything we are facing and feeling! He is here even in my experience of His absence.

This biblical teaching suggests something very important for the wounded woman. There is today such a tendency, both in our culture and sometimes in the church, to blame the victim. Rape victims hear it, abused women hear it, even mothers who have lost children hear it. It comes in many sophisticated forms and is often couched in spiritual overtones. The "blaming the victim routine" comes out in such phrases as, "But why didn't you lock your doors?" or "Why were you walking there?" or "How could you let your kids play there?" or "Couldn't you tell that your husband wasn't feeling well?"

All these remarks have the same undercutting assumption: "Your wounding is your fault . . . you got what you deserved." Although remarks of this nature may appear to be merely inquisitive or emanating from well-meaning concern, inherent in the question is an accusation that undercuts the dignity of pain and undermines the respect that ought to accompany the wounded state. Why is the victim made to feel the added burden of the emotional pain caused by suggesting that the tragedy or crime was partly the victim's fault?

Job's friends couldn't grant the dignity and legitimacy of Job's struggle with his loss. Three times the Apostle Paul asked God to take away his pain, until God revealed its special dignity. In pain and woundedness there exists a unique strength, a strength that comes to us in our weakness by means of God's grace (2 Corinthians 12:7-10). Women (as well as men) need to be affirmed in their feelings of woundedness, which can grant the rightful dignity to this stage of life. Pain should not be avoided, denied, or blamed, but embraced as a grace that strengthens us.

Even though we have these very specific promises about God's nearness to the widow in her need, the biblical perspective does not end here. As someone once said, "God's gotta' have arms." We find in Scripture not only promises of God's presence but also instruction as to how the community of believers should regard these wounded women.

## Care of the Widow Is Mandated

When God gave Israel its national constitution, He apparently foresaw all the potential realities the nation would face, and consequently compassionately imparted regulations to deal with these realities. Our God is a very realistic God, and as such doesn't live in some ivory tower. He knew property would be stolen, accidents would happen, people would go into debt, and husbands would die, thus creating widows and orphans.

Therefore, amidst the many ordinances, regulations, and commands, God placed the responsibility of caring for widows upon the community. Special offerings were to be taken for their care (Deuteronomy 14:28-29, 16:10-11), and the leftovers of harvest were to be left for them (24:17-22). Proper treatment of widows was seriously encouraged (Exodus 22:22), and mistreatment was a serious crime (Deuteronomy 27:19). When the prophets condemn Israel for its many crimes against God, one in particular stands at the forefront. The injustice and oppression toward innocents is high on the list of sins deserving severe judgment by God (Isaiah 1:17,23; 10:2; Ezekiel 22:7,25; Zechariah 7:10). In a sense, when God asks the nation to "shape up," He asks them to show mercy and stop oppressing the widows.

Again, the high regard God grants to this class of women in enjoining their care and protection to the nation tells us that this experience has extreme legitimacy. God Himself has validated the plight of the wounded by both encouraging proper care and condemning the oppression of those women who find themselves in severe need.

The New Testament only expands the concept of care. The physician Luke builds his two-volume account of the life of Christ and the early church around seven widows (Luke–Acts, with the symbolic number seven for completeness). He exalts the status of the widow by building or weaving his account of the life of Christ and the history of the early church around these episodes about widows.

The favor granted widows in the Gospel and Acts has become well-known: Anna, a widowed prophetess, who at age eighty-four is still awaiting the appearance of the Messiah (Luke 2:37); the widow of Nain, on whom Jesus takes compassion in raising her only son from the dead (Luke 7:12); our Lord's parable of the persistent widow as an illustration of prayer (Luke 18:1-8); the care of widows that had to be organized to keep the church free from racial bias (Acts 6:1); and Dorcas, a widow who apparently had an entire "order" or business employing other widows who specialized in doing good and helping the poor (Acts 9:39).

As in the Old Testament, the proper care of widows also becomes an issue in the early church. The Apostle Paul outlines several principles for governing the care of the needy in the church. First, he affirms all widows should be honored as mothers and sisters in the Lord (1 Timothy 5:3). Second, he believes widows should remain single unless they cannot control their sexual passion (1 Corinthians 7:8). If widows have living family members, either children or grandchildren, capable of caring for them, then the family members should assume the responsibility (1 Timothy 5:16).

Lastly, widows should be cared for by the church if they are "widows" indeed, and if they are over the age of sixty and known for their faithfulness in domestic and church ministry (1 Timothy 5:9-10). These may have been the first paid church staff! James, the brother of our Lord, concludes that the essence of religious devotion is caring for widows in their distress (James 1:27), thus affirming the necessity of caring for widows while acknowledging that not all widows are in distress. The widows who are to be cared for are those living in stress and need. Rather than being in need, some widows may in fact have more financial means than ever due to life insurance payments!

These passages assume that the wounded state, and the condition of need, is worthy of ministry and care. Moreover, the mere presence of so many commands and stern warnings about the treatment of widows indicates that widows were often neglected, ignored, mistreated, and ripped off. The community of the faithful is clearly commissioned to care for all the wounded in its midst. Scripture affirms the condition of the widow and grants a certain dignity to her feelings, but again the biblical portrait does not leave her in that condition.

### Benediction upon the Widow

The wounded woman can so withdraw into her pain and hurt that she may never come out again. Or she may come out like a hurt animal, embittered at life and God, attacking anyone with whom she comes into contact (Psalm 73:21-22). Or she may become a cantankerous, contentious woman who drives everyone out of her life (Proverbs 21:19).

Even though Scripture places a high regard on the plight of widows and asks the extended community of believers to care for the true widows, they also receive another special benediction. The widows who are commended in the Scripture are not commended for their feelings of woundedness; they are commended for their actions. A widow must move through her period of grief, and then appropriate and accept the loss as a part of her journey. She must do this in order to keep moving on in her life. This moving on is best characterized by moving out!

Consider Jesus' personal benediction on the widow who, having every right to justice simply as a widow, does not wait for others to defend her cause but takes it into her own hands. Jesus commends her "wearing out" the judge in an attempt to obtain her own justice (Luke 18:5). Widows had every right to obtain and live off the free-love offerings of Israel. On the very Temple compound where these resources were kept, Jesus commends a widow for giving all she had (Mark 12:41-44). It is this outward-moving, sacrificial self-giving of one who had every right to be receiving from others that Jesus draws attention to.

Anna, after only seven years of marriage, lost her husband. She apparently could have remarried, or pulled into her cave of pain and loss. But she used her widowed state as a time of praying, fasting, and waiting for the Messiah to make His presence known at the Temple. She waited for eighty-four years!

Yes, the biblical portrait of the widow is painted in all the dark, ominous tones of a person in legitimate pain. But the portrait doesn't remain dark. Radiant hues of color return as she begins her outward movement, doing whatever she can with what life has thrown at her. Widowhood is not, by far, the only pain experienced by women throughout their life's journey.

## OTHER WOUNDS WOMEN FACE

Woundedness can penetrate a woman's life at any age, and it can come from people she knows intimately or from strangers.[14] In addition to the woundedness caused by the death of a spouse or child, there are the traumas of childhood sexual and emotional abuse, rape, loss of employment, and divorce.

It is important to note that the pain of a woman who has suffered and experienced woundedness is very real and important to her. Her understanding of it is central to finding healing in order to progress forward in her journey with greater strength and maturity.

Viktor Frankl, philosopher and psychiatrist, wrote the classic book *Man's Search for Meaning*, in which he describes his imprisonment in a Nazi concentration camp and his search for why some survived and some did not. He concludes that pain is important to the one who suffers, even though some experiences are not as catastrophic as that of a prison camp. He writes:

> A man's (woman's) suffering is similar to the behavior of gas. If a certain quantity of gas is pumped into an empty chamber, it will fill the chamber completely and evenly, no matter how big the chamber. Thus, suffering completely fills the human soul and conscious mind, no matter whether the suffering is great or little. Therefore, the "size" of human suffering is absolutely relative.[15]

## Childhood Trauma

The emotional or physical abuse of children by parents is more widespread than most of us realize. Celebrities are coming forward and sharing their stories of childhood abuse. It is an interesting phenomenon, how we bury, hide, and deny such pain until a few brave souls come forward and reveal their experiences. Suddenly the floodgates open as women realize they are not alone, are not crazy, and can experience healing. When they have been given permission to share their abuse in the company of fellow sufferers, healing can begin to take place.

Our television talk shows have perhaps become overly inundated with the walking wounded, as talk-show hosts assume the role of lay psychologists. Some, I'm sure, do so as a part of their own healing process, and some exploit the pain of others for profit. The pendulum may have swung from too much silence to too much disclosure. Despite the overexposure, at least people are talking. Unfortunately, these televised wounded do not receive the answers or help they need. The television format is designed to make money, not heal people. It has become one huge commercial, marketing arena, where the wounded are paraded in front of rolling cameras. Bandages of simplistic solutions are offered to the bleeding, open wounds caused by long-term, complex problems. Meanwhile, behind the tears lies a programming format designed to sell detergent and toothpaste to its viewers.

Within the Christian community, there has been a reluctance and squeamishness to discuss child abuse. There seems to be an underlying assumption that when a Christian openly admits the effects of sin, whether it be child abuse, marital discord, or divorce, he or she is at fault for not trusting God or is guilty of walking in sin.

Why are we so afraid to admit our humanity and the frailness and pain that goes along with it? This admission certainly does not negate the power of God, or call into question the redemptive work of Christ in our lives. On the contrary, the devastating, destructive effects are well understood by our Lord, who bore the condemnation, pain, and alienation of our sins on the cross.

Sexual abuse of children is a most poignant issue that tugs at our hearts and has affected far more people than we realize. The shocking statistic that one out of every three women experiences sexual abuse at some point in her life is difficult to comprehend. Many did not recognize it as abuse at the time, since it occurred when they were too young to understand what was happening to them.

Dr. Dan Allender defines sexual abuse in his book *The Wounded Heart* as, "any contact or interaction (visual, verbal or psychological) between a child/adolescent and an adult when the child/adolescent is being used for the sexual stimulation of the perpetrator or any other person."[16]

What is heart-wrenching is the fact that physical abuse of children usually occurs at the hands of a family member or close associate of the family. A child is born into a family, helpless and totally dependent upon the parents for love, care, and protection. Sexual abuse by a parent violates and exploits that dependency, particularly when perpetrated against a young child.

Linda Sanford writes in *Strong at the Broken Places*, "The younger the victim, the more vulnerable she is. The more developmental skills and life experiences uncontaminated by trauma a child has, the more resources she has to draw on in the face of trauma."[17] The child is empty and defenseless, devoid of the necessary resources to understand the traumatic event that has happened. When most people experience trauma—a car accident, a plane crash, rape, war—there is always the need, in the aftermath of the event, to find safety and care. Imagine the bewilderment and terror of the sexually abused child who, for fear of betraying a parent or retaliation, is imprisoned behind a wall of silence and denial. In this condition healing is impossible, or at least improbable. Some women share that their mothers didn't want to hear about the abuse, called them a liar, or even worse, were an accessory to the abuse. This kind of neglectful and nonprotective mother is afraid to "rock the boat" in her own marriage relationship for fear of personal harm or abandonment. It is very probable that she too was abused as a child. A child does not get the opportunity to choose her parents, nor is the child held responsible for the way she is raised. A child enters into an already existing system and can easily become a vulnerable target upon which a parent can release his or her own personal pain.

Many children and adolescents are abused by someone outside the family unit. Usually it is a close associate of the family or a relative. Such was the case with Jean. As a young teenager, Jean was a quiet girl, growing up in a conservative, midwestern town. Her family was deeply involved in a church that communicated a negative "hellfire and brimstone" message that she says was more terrorizing than comforting.

With the arrival of a new pastor, the atmosphere at the church changed. His charming manner and positive preaching calmed Jean's fears as she found herself drawn to his messages of God's love and grace. Since this was a small church, the young pastor also served as youth pastor. Jean became more involved in youth activities, helping the pastor plan events and work around the office. Their activities took them to various events around the state, and soon this quiet, unassuming teenager was placed in an important, high-profile position as she assisted the pastor in his ministry.

During their times together, the pastor began to gradually make more physical advances toward Jean. Her lack of knowledge concerning sexual matters, her shyness, and her inexperience with boys left Jean in a highly vulnerable position. Her naiveté blinded her to the subtlety of his inappropriate sexual behavior. After all, who was she to argue or disagree with this powerful man of authority who had done so much for her? Jean felt like Eliza Doolittle in *My Fair Lady*, who was being transformed from an unnoticed duckling into a beautiful swan. She was his prodigy and he was going to make her into someone special.

From the age of fifteen to seventeen, Jean found herself becoming more physically involved with her pastor and feeling increasingly confused by everything. Jean never told anyone about her relationship with him. She was afraid of exposing this man as well as hurting his wife and children. Therefore, she carried the burden of abuse all alone. She tried to explain her apprehension and confusion to him, but he would pull out his Bible and spiritualize their actions. Jean was desperately trying to figure out how to get away from him, even if it meant leaving her hometown. Then the pastor died suddenly. Jean felt a strange mixture of grief and tremendous relief. She went on to live the next few years as your typical teenager, attending a Christian college and marrying a young man in the ministry.

It was not until years later that Jean found a "safe" confidant, and for the first time was able to share her secret. Her confidant's response was, "You were a child and that was child abuse." Jean said, "I thought I was having an affair because he said he loved me." As a result of the conversation with her friend, Jean was able, for the first time, to share her experience and begin to reframe it and understand it in a new light.

This began the process of healing for Jean. When she shared the experience with her husband, rather than showing concern about her, he became very angry. They had privately struggled in their marriage for years, while maintaining all the outward appearances of a spiritual couple in ministry. Jean had been disappointed in her relationship due to her husband's lack of emotional involvement in her life. Her fantasy dream of marriage had always been that her husband would ride into her life like a knight on a white horse to fill her every need and take care of her. As they began to talk over Jean's problem, it became clear that her husband also had hurts. He, too, had created a protective wall around his own feelings, leaving her on the outside.

For those who have been sexually abused, the feelings of shame, guilt, and responsibility for the abuse overshadow and affect every area of life. The child, and later the adult, creates a relational style of coping to protect himself or herself and maintain a sense of control. In *The Wounded Heart*, Allender described three general relational styles that he has commonly seen among women.

The first relational style is the "Good Girl." This is the woman who feels overly responsible for everyone, tries to do everything right, is competent, and gives sacrificially to those around her. The Good Girl feels "full of contempt . . . and will likely struggle with fantasies and sexualization of close relationships." This is what is going on inside. She is like a "house with the lights on, but never at home." She "allows only a small portion of pleasure or pain" and "is disengaged from most feelings except guilt." As a result, she experiences alienation and discord in her relationships. "The Good Girl is controlled, lonely, passive and full of self-contempt."

The second relational style is the "Tough Girl." This woman maintains control and independence through a tough exterior wall of emotional detachment, defensiveness, and hostility. Inside, she is "above her own feelings, suspicious of others' motives, arrogant and angry in her evaluations of others." Her prickly edge, impenetrability, and control make the Tough Girl a lonely woman.

The third woman is the "Party Girl." "She is usually fragile and funny, sincere and phony, blunt and dishonest—a series of paradoxes." Her outward approach is one of a fickle and seductive manner, while inwardly she fears the intimacy and commitment of a relationship. She is a needy woman, insatiable in her desires and demanding in her love life, which ultimately becomes parasitic.

> The three styles of relating can be briefly summarized: the Good Girl is committed to pleasure and relief through faithful attendance to relationship; the Tough Girl, to the exercise of power through control and intimidation; the Party Girl, to enmeshment and control through seductive lust and/or guilt.[18]

Jean fit the relational style of the Good Girl, playing the role of the perfect wife and mother to the outside world while angry and hurt on the inside. Her efforts to make everyone happy and bear the emotional responsibility for those around her took her to a breaking point where she finally gave up. As she read the story of Abraham's willingness to sacrifice Isaac on the altar to God, she realized that she, too, had a sacrifice to make. Jean relinquished her fantasy of the "ideal marriage" and gave up her sense of control and responsibility. She experienced a welcome sense of release, and her husband experienced the absence of pressure to perform. The struggles are still there, but now they are both better equipped to deal with them. They now acknowledge the very real presence of a sin nature and appreciate God's grace and forgiveness to a greater degree.

God has used this couple to touch the lives of others. As they share in other people's pain, they offer hope and comfort based on their own experiences and the faithfulness of God. They have learned the reality expressed by the prophet:

> Why has my pain been perpetual
> And my wound incurable, refusing to be healed?
> Wilt Thou indeed be to me like a deceptive stream
> With water that is unreliable?
> Therefore, thus says the LORD,
> "If you return, then I will restore you—
> Before Me you will stand;
> And if you extract the precious from the worthless,
> You will become My spokesman." (Jeremiah 15:18-19)

It is impossible to adequately deal with the depth and complexity of physical and emotional child abuse. This is a wound that leaves scars for a lifetime. A woman must first break down the walls of silence and denial as she acknowledges her trauma. Through a support group and/or sensitive counselor, it is possible for the adult to face the pain of the child within and reframe the abuse. There is the need to alleviate the shame, guilt, and responsibility one feels for the abuse. The child was not responsible for what happened. However, the adult woman is now responsible for what she does with her childhood—to make peace with it and move out of her woundedness.

First, a woman's pain must be validated. Then, she must mourn appropriately for the loss of childhood innocence. She must then deal with the inappropriate behaviors she has learned as coping mechanisms and embrace the necessary forgiveness of the perpetrator in order to find peace. Abuse is another fork in the road of life to which one must backtrack in order to set out on a better path. If a woman does not return to the abuse, she can get stuck at this wounded stage. There is no going on without going back!

## Loss of a Woman's Marriage

The woundedness of divorce more closely resembles the pain and bereavement of death than any other life event. As a matter of fact, divorce is a death. It is the untimely and unnatural termination of a life. Although no person has died, a death has taken place. What has died? The life of the marriage.

A man and a woman come together physically and produce a child. Likewise, as the couple commits to each other emotionally, psychologically, physically, and spiritually, a relationship is born. This relationship is nourished, cared for, and protected; it goes through various growth stages similar to that of a child. It is important that a woman who is experiencing divorce understand the concept of the death of this living relationship. This understanding will explain her passage through the stages of grief and her emotional upheaval.

Many books have been written on divorce, both from a theological and practical viewpoint. It is not my intention to deal with the appropriateness or ethics of divorce. Divorce is a reality. George Barna writes in *The Future of the American Family* that "America now boasts the highest divorce rate in the world."[19] He also claims that the statistic that 50 percent of marriages end in divorce is unreasonably high. His research has shown that "only about one-fourth of Americans who have been married also experienced at least one divorce."[20] Barna goes on to state that "two out of three second or subsequent marriages eventually fail."[21] Divorce runs its devastating course and "inflicts damage on all population groups with nearly equal frequency and ferocity." Divorce, like death, is no respecter of persons!

One of the classic books on divorce is *Second Chances*, by Judith Wallerstein. The uniqueness of this book is that it is the first long-term study undertaken, researching the effects of divorce on men, women, and especially children. Wallerstein writes,

> Divorce has ripple effects that touch not just the family involved, but our entire society. Pat Conroy observed when his own marriage broke up, "Each divorce is the death of a small civilization." When one family divorces, that divorce affects relatives, friends, neighbors, employers, teachers, clergy and scores of strangers. Although more people stay married than get divorces, divorce is not a "them" versus "us" problem; everyone, in one way or another, has been touched by it.[22]

### The Effects of Divorce

The loss of identity and self-esteem are deeply felt in divorce. As previously discussed, a woman's identity is defined within the context of her connection to those around her and her ability to care for these relationships. A woman's marriage contains the greatest investment of her time, efforts, emotions, and commitment. Its dissolution has the power to totally uproot her adult identity. Divorce is like the severing of a limb. It is losing a part of you. It hurts. Usually men are not as devastated by divorce as women are. Although a family is important to a man, it is not the primary place from which he derives his identity.

Because of the woman's investment in her marriage, she carries the guilt, emotional loss, and responsibility for the divorce much more readily than her husband does. Women hold the market share on guilt. Men feel a sense of failure in their responsibility. Some men experience the loss of their marriage in the same way they do the loss of their business. For others, the reality is that the loss of a job may be more devastating than the loss of a marriage. "For a host of reasons, men undergo less psychological change than women in the wake of divorce."[23] However, while women feel it is their fault that the marriage failed, research shows that the divorce is a result of a variety of complex issues. Barna writes:

Our research suggests that the most serious of the problems that lead to divorce are different core values between the partners, poor communication, financial tension and selfishness. Although adultery has a high likelihood of causing a divorce, being caught in an adulterous relationship is not as common as these other problems.[24]

A woman is wounded by the drastic change in her economic position due to the divorce. Steven Nock writes in *Sociology of the Family*:

Many women who had not worked before now enter the labor force. Many of those who are employed now must stretch their earnings much further than before. Wives who are awarded some child support by the courts soon realize that such payments from their ex-husbands are inadequate and are a source of continual conflict (often placing the ex-wife in the position of having to appeal to her ex-husband for additional help). For both men and women, the financial burdens caused by divorce add yet one more dimension to already shaken self-images and further challenge the sense of being able to make it on one's own.[25]

Some of the possible economic repercussions include the sale of a woman's home; relocation to another city; the radical drop in lifestyle; and the loss of her credit history, which is usually in the husband's name. According to Wallerstein's research, as a result of divorce "half the men were solidly upper or middle class while, with few exceptions, women were poorer."[26]

My reading and our relationships with Christian couples for the last twenty-five years affirm the sad but true fact that Christians fail in marriage just as nonChristians do. No one is immune to marital struggles or guaranteed the promise of success. Barna's research revealed that the role of religion played a minor role throughout the divorce procedure. Religion did not provide the expected comfort and strength. While many people retained their religious beliefs after the divorce, their church attendance declined due to lack of church support and judgmental attitudes.[27]

Judy had been married to a successful businessman for over ten years when she discovered he was having an affair. Feelings of terror and devastation permeated her being. She said, "All I could see was my security evaporating and leaving me with nothing. I had invested too many years in this relationship, had three small children, and was terrified of going back to work. I hadn't worked in years." Her life had been wrapped up in her husband. Although he was a dominating man, she said, "He was all I knew." She attributed his affair to a mid-life crisis. Maybe it would pass. He said he loved her and that the affair was over. The two of them began attending counseling. Judy thought things were improving as her trust toward her husband began to slowly rebuild. However, Judy wisely sought legal counsel and decided to go back to school and prepare herself for a career.

Several years went by before Judy became aware that her husband was having another affair. Once again he told her that he still loved her. However, after a third affair, Judy consulted a lawyer and began divorce proceedings. At this point, Judy said she was no longer terrified at the prospect of a divorce, just sad. I asked Judy what role her faith played during this difficult time. She quietly commented, "I became very disappointed in God. I was in a good Bible study and tried to do what the Bible said. It just didn't work."

Judy's experience is like that of many women who feel they have been abandoned by God during the painful process of marital strife and divorce. I talked with a counselor friend about the uniqueness of a Christian woman's response to an unfaithful or abusive husband as opposed to a nonChristian woman's. The Christian doctrine of the sanctity of marriage creates a tremendous sense of responsibility toward the marriage and a deep desire to honor God through it. Christian women who are living with abusive or unfaithful husbands endure far too much for fear of being labeled unsubmissive and disobedient. My reading has included several examples of women who were told that it was God's will to stay in the marriage and they would just have to make it work.

I do not believe divorce is God's will nor would I counsel a woman toward it. However, I feel strongly that a woman must protect herself physically and emotionally from a destructive husband. Any woman who finds herself in this position should seek help immediately from those who can understand and support her position, not judge her spirit. If a woman's physical safety is at risk, she should leave her husband for a period of time while a course of action is determined. Too many women are dying a slow death and need help.

## Loss of Employment

Loss of employment is another wound many women face today. It has become an increasingly common experience for both men and women in our society. Our changing economy and the instability of the corporate world due to leveraged buy-outs, mergers, and downsizing have brought a strong sense of insecurity, betrayal, and fear to the workplace. The consistent rise in the cost of living and the pursuit of the American dream, to which we all feel entitled, leave us stressed and living on the edge. Gone are the days when people worked for the same company for thirty to forty years, secure with health-care and retirement benefits. Gone are the days when people were able to save a substantial amount of income to put their kids through college and provide for their own comfortable "golden years." For many people, one to six months without a paycheck would put them under. It is estimated that the average worker will change jobs over seven times in his lifetime, several of these being to an entirely new vocation. Is it any wonder that the tenuousness of job security has created a land of "walking wounded" among both men and women?

Baby boomers have been caught in a maelstrom of political, economic, and social changes. The roles of men and women are more complex and changing than ever before. No longer is the traditional home one in which the husband is the primary provider and the wife is a stay-at-home mother. More couples are choosing a two-paycheck home where both husband and wife work. Due to the rise in divorce, more women are forced into the marketplace to meet their own financial obligations or replace the loss of the husband's income. The influence of the women's movement has resulted in better educated women who have more options than women in the past. They can now enter the previously male-dominated worlds of corporate life, politics, sports, professional fields, and small business. Some women are opting for the single life, reserving the option of marriage and family for later in their lives.

Regardless of the path a woman chooses, job security for herself and/or her husband is critical. Social pressure to be successful, the strain of financial goals mixed with professional expectations, and the stigma of unemployment set one up for a tremendous amount of trauma created by the loss of work. The loss of employment cuts through the life of each of us. The crisis of job loss shatters our basic assumptions about ourselves and life. It challenges our relationships, exposes our vulnerabilities, jeopardizes our self-esteem, and thrusts us from independence into dependency.

### Loss of the Husband's Job

For women who want the traditional way of life, the loss of a husband's employment threatens their sense of security, disrupts their lifestyle, and impedes their opportunity to be the ever-present caregiver to their children. It also can severely expose the weaknesses and inadequacies of their marriage partners as well as their over-dependence on their husbands.

These changes can create opportunities for growth, a greater sense of shared responsibility, and a more experiential dependency upon the provisions of God. A family going through the trauma of unemployment can achieve new levels of intimacy and maturity. As each family member is stretched and has to learn new roles and responsibilities, the family develops a greater sense of interdependence.

A woman can uncover her often unused, latent talents, or find a renewed confidence in her own abilities. Some women describe an increased emotional resiliency and praise the newfound opportunities for personal development apart from their families. The reality of a woman's life anyway is that one day the children will leave, and her life will need a new direction and focus. There is also the likelihood of outliving her mate. Unemployment of the husband may be the time to accept and prepare for the inevitable changes of the future.

### The Woundedness of a Woman's Unemployment

This new generation of women, having been influenced by the massive social changes of the sixties and the women's movement, approaches life far differently than their mothers did. This new breed of woman graduates from college and takes off running in pursuit of a career rather than a family. She has a myriad of options ahead of her. Her role model may no longer be her mother but the woman CEO of some successful company. She no longer finds her identity by attaching her star to a man and buying in to his dreams for success. She has her own ambitions and her own dreams, which may or may not include a husband and children. This woman is not only defined by the relationships around her but also by the work that she does.

People used to work for personal security, now they work for personal significance. "The movement from an industrial society to a technological society creates the drive for finding more meaning in work than work could ever provide. Achievement, recognition, status, style and affluence became the 'hype' words of the seventies and eighties."[28]

As a result, the woundedness a woman will experience through the loss of her job is as devastating to her sense of identity as that experienced by a man.

Whitney has been a working woman from the time she graduated from college. Although married, she has invested herself primarily in her career and its advancement. Whitney admitted, "Home was just a place I passed through on my way to work. I felt more connected to my job than I did to my home."

Whitney's husband was in graduate school, allowing her to devote herself to work. She was putting in ten- to twelve-hour days, six days a week. She enjoyed being a workaholic. Therefore, when Whitney lost her job, she was devastated. "I was surprised by the range of emotions I felt. I felt like I had been punched in the stomach and experienced the classic stages of grief." She explained, "I felt betrayed. One day you're a part of this happy family and the next day you're told you are no longer a part of the family." Whitney assumed if she worked hard and was productive she would be rewarded. According to her way of thinking, "People don't lose their job unless they screw up." Suddenly, her contributions and hard work seemed worthless and meaningless. For the first time, feelings of low self-esteem and negative self-talk hammered away in her mind. Her career track had suddenly hit a roadblock, and she felt totally frustrated and powerless.

When Whitney went home to share the news with her parents, their reaction was another nail in the coffin. Rather than finding comfort and understanding, she found blame. Her mother's initial response was, "What did you do wrong?" Her mother had never worked outside the home and had no appreciation for what this loss represented to Whitney. Her father had worked for the same company for thirty-five years and had no comprehension of the pain of being fired. They assumed it was her fault that she lost her job. It was a classic blame-the-victim response.

As she began the painful and tedious process of a job search, Whitney discovered both family and friends to be of little comfort. She commented, "They just don't know how to act around an unemployed person." She isolated herself from others as she continued to be plagued by a trail of negative thoughts, a wounded self-esteem, and doubt.

However, as a Christian, Whitney found herself drawn to the Word of God, seeking His perspective and comfort. Through a study of God's perspective on work and reading such books as *Your Work Matters to God*, by Doug Sherman and Bill Hendricks, Whitney developed a new mind-set concerning the meaning of work. She realized that she, like so many in the workplace, had assigned to work a significance and meaning that far surpassed God's purpose for it in their lives.

What is work? The dictionary is full of different meanings. Let's keep it simple by saying "that work is whatever we do to sustain ourselves in the world. From this definition, it should be clear that work involves far more than a mere job or occupation. It involves our goals, our time, our motives, and ultimately our view of life and ourselves."[29] The reality is that work not only provides one with the means to make a living, but it also brings a greater sense of dignity and hopefully some measure of enjoyment (Ecclesiastes 5:18-19). "Through work we serve people, through work we meet our own needs, through work we meet our family's need, through work we earn money to give to others, through work we love God."[30]

Women in the workplace will face the battle that men have fought for years. They will find themselves grappling not only with the seduction of power but with the wounds it inflicts. Working women are blazing a new trail through what has previously been men's territory. Pioneers in any endeavor, if they aren't killed in the process, usually arrive with a few arrows in their back. Women have to work harder than men in many cases to gain the recognition and respect they deserve, forcing men to take them seriously.

Some of the wounds of work are: overwork, neglect of personal health, the conflict of career and children, friction within their own marriage, misunderstanding by men, loss of femininity, and aloneness. "Women recognize that there really has been no support. It's not only lonely at the top, it is lonely on every rung of the ladder for a lot of women."[31] The woundedness of the workplace is a reality. With God's grace, a woman will benefit from the mentoring and modeling of others who encourage her endeavors and occasionally help her pull out the arrows.

## EMBRACE THE TRIALS

It is an interesting phenomenon of human nature that losses catch us humans by such surprise. Jesus Himself told us that "in the world you have tribulation" (John 16:33). We are also told by James to "consider it all joy, my brethren, when you encounter various trials" (1:2). In other words, as we journey down the path of life, we will occasionally stumble or fall into difficult situations. The Bible tells us to embrace these trials as we would a long-lost friend who unexpectedly appears at our door. It is one thing to give casual, intellectual assent to this recommendation, but quite another to actually do it.

At first, this seems an inappropriate and unnatural response to trauma, loss, and grief. If one has experienced the shock of a death, the agony of long-term suffering, the reality of divorce, or the shattering of a dream, this response probably seems impossible and even crazy! However, James goes on to say, "[Know] that the testing of your faith produces endurance. And let endurance have its perfect result, that you may be perfect and complete, lacking in nothing" (1:3-4). James seems to be saying that our response of faith and acceptance of this trial, not negating the emotional pain and grieving process, may ultimately result in a moving forward and growth in our character.

You may find yourself saying, "If this is character building, then I can do without character! With friends like this, who needs enemies?" This "endurance" or "work" that is taking place may bring a maturity to our lives that will reflect more of the perfection and wholeness of Christ. This goes back to the statement that "we grow by giving up" in Viorst's book.

As Christian women, we long to be imitators of Christ in our lives. This means to live life fully, respond to life, and impact life in such a way that indicates the presence and power of Christ within us. The prophet Isaiah wrote that the Messiah would be "a man of sorrows, and acquainted with grief." He goes on to say,

> Surely our griefs He Himself bore,
> And our sorrows He carried. (Isaiah 53:4)

Jesus was no stranger to trials, suffering, and death. However, there was a specific meaning and purpose in His death, for

> The LORD has caused the iniquity of us all
> To fall on Him. (verse 6)

Therefore,

The LORD was pleased
To crush Him, putting Him to grief;
If He would render Himself as a guilt offering. (verse 10)

Jesus paid the penalty for man's shortcomings so that we would have access to God and spend eternity with Him. The writer to the Hebrews commends this perfecting through suffering: "Although He was a Son, He learned obedience from the things which He suffered. And having been made perfect, He became to all those who obey Him the source of eternal salvation" (Hebrews 5:8-9).

I am eternally grateful that Jesus was willing to be wounded on my behalf and die in my place. I find comfort in realizing He was a real flesh-and-blood Person who struggled with His pain. As the dark night of His betrayal was unfolding, He prayed in the garden, "My Father, if it is possible, let this cup pass from Me; yet not as I will, but as Thou wilt" (Matthew 26:39). In this one statement, we see both the human and divine natures at work in our Messiah.

The reality that death is essential to the fulfillment of God's purposes for man is a stark and graphic reminder of how God views wounding. His own Son stands throughout history as the fallen, betrayed Innocent. He knows a victimization that no woman can ever imagine. From His wounds flows not only His blood but our life. The reality is clear, there can be no forward movement, no path toward maturity without the pain of wounding. It is an essential element of the life we live. Cells must die in order to be replaced by newer living ones. Seeds must be planted in dark soil in order to "die" and bring forth a harvest (John 12:24). As Viorst confesses, "We live by losing and leaving and letting go. And sooner or later, with more or less pain, we all must come to know that loss is indeed a lifelong human condition."[32]

What emerges out of this time of pain is a much stronger woman, a woman more in touch with who she is and what is really important to her. Let's face it, Helen Reddy was right when she sang about "Woman."[33] A woman's wisdom is a wisdom born in pain. In the places where she was broken, she becomes stronger.

CHAPTER SEVEN

# THE WOMAN OF STRENGTH: A STEEL MAGNOLIA

❦

*Men are taught to apologize for their weakness,*
*Women for their strengths.*
LOIS WYSE

*I've always believed in the adage that the secret*
*of eternal youth is arrested development.*
ALICE ROOSEVELT LONGWORTH

I thoroughly enjoyed the movie *Steel Magnolias*, even though it had certain limitations. The storyline revolves around six women living in a small southern town. Their lives are bound together through the years by sharing the joys and sorrows of everyday life, as well as putting up with each other's idiosyncrasies.

The movie title uses the fragrant, large, white magnolia flower to symbolize the femininity of these women. The word *steel* refers to the strength developed and required to survive the blows of life. "Steel" used in this way does not suggest that these women were tough or hardened, but rather they were women of proven character and inner strength. The title, *Steel Magnolias*, then seems an oxymoron, combining contradictory ideas or terms.

As I approached this final chapter, I felt this oxymoron was a fitting description of the last season of a woman's life.[1] As a woman approaches the end of her earthly journey, there is the hope that her life will be marked by maturity. However, the important question to ask is, "What does maturity look like?"

In the field of human development, various theorists have set forth the differing ideal ends or goals of human development. Each theory centers on the question of what constitutes the mature or totally grown-up person. Erickson argues that the goal of adult

163

development is to arrive as a mature adult with a certain "generativity and integrity." For Levinson, the goal is to arrive in mid-life with a certain stability and meaning to one's commitments and values.[2] Kohlberg, the guru of the moral development school, says the goal is to have a fully developed moral conscience. In these stages of moral development, the mature conscience is described as one having the ability to do acts of righteousness as based on well-articulated, universal, ethical principles.[3] Gilligan alludes to the female adult development whereby a woman gains "a new understanding of the connection between herself and others which is articulated by the concept of responsibility."[4] For Maslow, the final stage is to be a fully functioning human being (fully self-actualized), and in Fowler's development the truly mature individual is the person whose faith is no longer influenced by his or her primary outside groups but by the imperatives of love and justice.[5]

Each of these theorists has contributed a way of understanding what the aim or direction of one's life journey should be and, in a sense, where it should end. Even though it seems to me their ideas are still fairly lofty, abstract, and difficult to see in real-life human beings, their ideas are worth contemplating. What is even more fascinating is that what they have described as the final destination of an adult's life is very similar to an ancient acrostic.[6]

This Hebrew acrostic closes out a section of the wisdom literature in the Old Testament. The book of Proverbs presents many different types of characters that a person will run into during his or her journey. People such as the sluggard, the fool, the naive, the scoffer, the wicked, the adulterous woman, the wise woman, and of course, the infamous contentious woman. But throughout this book is another woman, the one called Wisdom. This woman implores the youth of the nation to come, learn from her, and be influenced by her words (Proverbs 8:1-36). Wisdom, personified as a woman, builds her home, sends out her emissaries, and counsels the naive, scoffers, and fools to forsake their folly (Proverbs 1:20-33, 9:4-6).

This extended counsel on the merits of wisdom over foolishness, couched in pithy proverbs, concludes with a tribute to this woman of wisdom. It is my understanding of this literature that the closing tribute functioned in much the same way as the final stage in most developmental theories. This woman of wisdom was the goal for young women to pursue and seek to emulate. For those who did not have the kind of mother, or women in their locale, to look at as role models, this literary acrostic played a very important role. A woman could read it and have a picture of what the mature woman was all about.

In many ways, I think this portrait is far clearer than most of the rather high-sounding abstractions the researchers have produced. To me, the phrase "she extends her hand to the poor" is far clearer than "having a universalized, principlized set of ethical moral imperatives." They may say the same thing, but I get the point much clearer in the first phrase. Maybe this is because I am not totally "abstracted" yet!

I believe that in this concluding tribute to a woman, Proverbs gives us the final stage on the woman's journey. It is the stage of final maturity and wisdom. But don't let the reading of this passage throw you. Many young women read it and are either compulsively driven by it, or totally overwhelmed by this woman's talents. It seems she is the superwoman that all women are supposed to be. She appears to have it all. Trying to emulate this woman can be very defeating and unrealistic! I believe, however, that a proper reading of this extended poem reveals the very feminine-journey motif discussed in this book. It portrays certain stages in a woman's life that are characterized by certain defining attributes. But first, some comments about what this woman is to be called.

## A WOMAN OF WHAT?

The various translations of the Hebrew term *'eshet hayil* are somewhat humorous. The *New American Standard Bible* reads, "the excellent wife"; *The New International Version*, "a wife of noble character"; the *King James Version*, "the virtuous woman"; and the *New English Bible*, "a capable woman." All of these translations are wrestling with the fundamental problem of how to put into English what the term *hayil* conveys.

First and foremost, the Hebrew term *hayil*, translated as "excellent, virtuous, noble and capable," is a power term. As a noun, it is used throughout the Old Testament with the meanings of "strength, ability, wealth and the massing of armies."[7] It is used of physical strength in the passage, "The bows of the mighty are shattered, but the feeble gird on strength [*hayil*]" (1 Samuel 2:4).

It is also used of the strength of a horse (Psalm 33:17) and of mighty men of valor. The word *valor* translates *hayil* (Judges 6:12,

1 Samuel 9:1, 2 Kings 5:1). *Hayil* also carries the ideas of "having certain abilities . . . with livestock" (Genesis 47:6), the moral commitment of fearing God and hating dishonesty (Exodus 18:21,25), being driven by moral convictions rather than youthful passions (Ruth 3:11), and having obtained a royal position (1 Kings 1:42,52).

*Hayil* is often used of men of wealth and status (Genesis 34:29; Deuteronomy 8:17-18; Psalm 49:7,11; Isaiah 8:4), as well as groups of strong, armed men involved in protecting royalty and the nation (Exodus 14:4,9,17; 1 Samuel 17:20; 1 Kings 15:20; 2 Kings 18:17; Ezekiel 27:11). Finally, this term is used of God's attributes and one He imparts to His children (Psalm 18:32,39; 60:12; 108:13; 118:15; Habakkuk 3:19). In these passages, the central idea is God's valiant victory, which He performs for the sake of the righteous. In other places, it is the special strength or ability God gives to His people in order that they might do valiantly.

In summary, this word is not easily translatable, as the translations illustrate. In general, the word carries the ideas of strength and power. The usage of *hayil* is more commonly found of men and especially military warriors and armed men. Sometimes the meaning is more appropriately connected with "special forces" or reconnaissance units who "spy out the land" (Judges 18:2).

With reference to the meaning of "wealth," the term is again normally used of men such as Boaz, who owned property, or men who, because of their abundance of silver, were asked to donate it (2 Kings 15:20). Ruth is, uncharacteristically, called a woman of *hayil*, or "standing in the community," because of the status she had obtained by bearing children. They have become her monetary worth (Ruth 4:11)! This perspective is confirmed when Solomon refers to children as a heritage from the Lord (Psalm 127:3). All of this background must be brought to bear when looking at this final stage of the woman's journey.

The question must be raised, "What is this *'eshet hayil* a woman of?" The book of Proverbs uses this term four times, two of which are in this acrostic tribute. The first of the other two usages is found in 12:4—"An excellent wife is the crown of her husband, but she who shames him is as rottenness in his bones."

In a Jewish commentary on the role of Jewish women, this verse is translated "a valiant woman," which is more consistent with the translations of *hayil* when used of men.[8] Whatever this woman is, she is the sterling crown to her husband's head. In the parallelism of the

Hebrew poetry, her "strength, excellence, or valor" is expressed in not bringing shame to her husband. This idea fits nicely with this phrase: "She does him good and not evil all the days of her life" (31:12).

In the other passage, the mother of King Lemuel offers her son some maternal advice. She says, "Do not give your strength [*hayil*] to women, or your ways to that which destroys kings" (31:3). This, perhaps, picks up the nuance of ability or regal powers that are to be used for the protection of the needy and the afflicted. Indeed, the power of the throne can be thrown away and wasted when indulgence in ungodly women and wine becomes the norm (31:5-9).

An example of this verse is the current marital situation in England between Prince Charles and Princess Diana. Their pending divorce and inability to maintain their marriage is creating an instability and weakening of the royal family's power. A divorce would prohibit Prince Charles from assuming the role of king of England. He is losing the power that he has spent a lifetime preparing for.

Admitting that it is very difficult to translate this term, I will just call her "a woman of strength." This carries with it a certain irony, since women through various historical periods have not been described by the word *strength*. The Victorian woman was anything but strong. Words like *virtuous*, *frail*, *demure*, and *dependent* fit her image far better. Even today, some in various kinds of churches would be offended, if not outraged, to think of women as powerful. Those who admit to her power may see this attribute in the negative and certainly not as a virtue. They would consider it as a threat to the leadership role of men. Whatever the case, my simple translation is, "woman of strength or power." At each stage of a woman's journey as described by this poem, strength is seen as her defining attribute.

Her strength of character and her growing abilities increase with age, until she receives the fullness of praise at her late-in-life destination. The adulation and virtue many woman are seeking today may only be seen at life's end and not at the beginning or middle. Women may be, in fact, wanting too much, too early in this regard. If life is a journey, and I believe it is, we as women may be in too much of a hurry. Those of us from the baby-boomer generation feel a sense of entitlement or reward while ignoring the process and the price for its obtainment. We cannot reap that which we have not sown. The goal of being a woman is to find our tribute much later in life than we currently expect it. So what does it mean to be a woman of strength?

## A WOMAN OF REFLECTION

The writer of Proverbs first shows the *'eshet hayil* reflecting upon her life in its various seasons. A fitting introduction sets the stage: A strong woman who can find? (31:10). The implication being that this kind of woman is indeed a rare commodity. The recognition exists that not all women are such, or will even seek to be of such character. Within Proverbs itself this recognition exists. The continual presence of the adulterous, foolish, and contentious woman suggests that this woman of strong, godly character is a rare breed (14:1, 21:19, 27:15, 30:20). For whatever reasons, many women do not seek or live out the realities of the strong woman. But she still is the goal for the women who desire such.

The writer also recognizes the long-standing foundation of the strong woman's primary relationship, her marriage. For those of you who are single, you may find it difficult to identify with aspects of this woman's life. Although marriage and family are the norm for most women, it is not the experience of all women. If a woman is married, God will use the marriage relationship as the primary developer of maturity in her life. If she is not married, God will use other relationships and events also to bring that woman to maturity.

As a wife looks back on her life, she realizes, as a mature woman, that there existed a certain interpersonal benevolence with her husband. It was a reciprocal relationship whereby trust and doing good fed each other in positive ways. The wife has reached a sense of peace and acceptance concerning her husband, a far cry from the young wife bent on changing him. The husband trusts in his wife's abilities with the same kind of reliable security and safety he places in God. The benefit to him is that he has no need to go outside of this relationship to find the special toys or masculine plunder to excite his life. The riches of his wife are enough![9]

The single woman should approach all of her relationships with both male and female friends within this same framework of trust. The mature woman does not play games with the lives and feelings of others or manipulate them in a self-serving way.

A smart wife deals with her husband bountifully by doing him good all the days of her life. Again, the term "deals bountifully" picks up the language the psalmists use to talk about the bounty God gives to the righteous (Psalm 13:6, 116:7, 119:17, 142:7). Therefore, as this woman late in life reflects on her marriage, she can see (in spite of the trials and conflicts) a certain disposition of benevolence that was always underneath the daily grind.

The second aspect of the reflection deals with her memory of the early years (Proverbs 31:13-17). During these years, the woman's strength is seen in the context of her home. These are the high-energy years, when the main contribution of a woman with children is seen in the lives of those who grace her home. Her time is spent in providing, planning, and producing. She becomes skilled in obtaining the necessary commodities for her family and extended helpers! She uses her mental acumen to research and plot a course of action to obtain a field.[10] Having tracked it down and purchased it, she develops a vineyard. At this point, some see her entering the world of business, but the text seems to indicate that the purchase is primarily for the sake of providing for her family. Her business endeavors will come later! The productivity of the vineyard is not for corporate profit but for the care of her home.

This season of her life concludes with the statement that her main apparel is strength.[11] This woman of ability is characterized during these early years not by her luxurious clothing but by her stamina and strength. Her arms are not the pale, fragile limbs of the pampered Victorian woman, but the well-worn arms of an involved, busy domestic. Strength of body and strength of character are her defining and distinctive attributes (verse 17).

According to *Megatrends For Women*, "Working at home is the dream of the '90's." Women have experienced the same burnout in the workplace as men but are not as willing to sacrifice their families for their careers. Today, women desire more balance between work and family and are looking for creative work alternatives. As a result, "The number of self-employed women working full time at home tripled between 1985 and 1991, from 378,000 to 1.1 million."[12]

Jacqueline is one of the many young mothers who works full-time out of her home. She loves her work as a book publicist and has dreams of one day expanding into her own public relations agency and printing company. She has been tempering certain career aspirations because of the demanding responsibilities of motherhood. However, she is grateful for the opportunity to be at home with her two young sons while pursuing her career and financial goals.

Let's face it, what women like Jacqueline are doing today demands strength, both physical and mental. As the mature women reflects upon these earlier years, what she and others remember is her strength manifested in her home.

After this reflection, she then moves on to consider her middle years. At this point, the text takes on a tone of self-evaluation (verse 18). From her mid-life perspective she analyzes her experience thus far. This is a precarious time for many women. Gail Sheehy notes, "More than anything else, it is our own view of ourselves that determines the richness or paucity of the middle years."[13] Many women bail out at this point. Having tasted enough of life, they draw permanent conclusions—some good, others not so good—about the way they think life is. The woman of strong character confesses that what she has tasted and experienced is essentially good.[14]

I'm sure much had happened in this woman's life that she did not consider good at the time, but from her mid-life vantage point she examines it for its hidden benefit. What is interesting about this evaluation is that without a positive reframing of the most evil of experiences, one can never adequately recover.[15] To look back on one's life at this juncture is serious business. The temptation lies in comparison. As a woman compares her life with other women's lives, there can be a frightening realization that she has missed the best of life. Her house is not as nice or as big as her best friend's; her husband's job is not as secure or high-paying as someone in another profession; other women's kids have gotten into Ivy League colleges, and married rich; some of them seem to have achieved more spiritual success. A gnawing dissatisfaction can set in at this time of life that makes a woman look back with regret. When she evaluates the first twenty or so years, all she sees are her mistakes, misfortunes, and missed opportunities.

In contrast, the woman of strength values her earlier years and sees them as granting her favorable gain (verse 18). For example, women who have been through a divorce, says Wallerstein, can choose to either waste their experience or gain by it. She writes,

> The danger in every crisis is that people will remain in the same place, continuing through the years to react to initial impact as if it had just struck. The opportunities in every crisis are for people to rebuild what was destroyed or to create a reasonable substitute; to be able to grow emotionally, establish a new competence and pride; and to strengthen intimate relationships far beyond earlier capacities.[16]

For those women left in the devastating wake of a divorce and possibly the added responsibiliy of single parenting, life seems overwhelming. It will take time and effort to regain your footing and for the pain to heal. The good news is that there is life after divorce. God is the master of restoring life (Ezekiel 37:1-14). He is able to strengthen and build a life with more meaning and productivity than you ever thought possible.

At this point in the development, the strong woman recommits herself to the actions that have brought her this far. Her life during "middle-essence" is characterized by continued profitability, availability, hospitality, and charity with more productivity. What describes her life in this season is not the social withdrawal sometimes common to older women, but an outward movement toward her work, the needs of society, and her own household. She is not idle but keeps her lamp burning at night (Proverbs 31:18) as an invitation to the traveler of her hospitality, while also laboring with her hands (verse 19). Rather than being only concerned with her own interests, she also looks to the needs of others. She takes a personal interest in "spreading out" her assets to assist those in need (verse 20),[17] while also taking care of her own needs (verse 22). She has learned that taking care of herself is not in opposition to providing the necessary resources for her loved ones. She makes clothes for herself as well as for others (verse 22). Whereas in her earlier years her clothing was her energetic strength of character, now she is clothed with fine linen and purple.

As I read this passage and considered a present-day example of a woman who spent the latter part of her life looking to the needs of others, the actress Audrey Hepburn came to mind. She was honored in the wake of her untimely death in January 1993 at the age of sixty-three due to cancer. Her picture was on the cover of *Life* magazine, and a statement made about her caught my attention. One of her previous directors wrote, "She looked like a princess in a fairy tale, a Dresden figurine with huge, soulful eyes. But there was steel beneath the porcelain, an aristocratic rigor that shaped every gesture with integrity and taste."[18] The contrast between the fragile, porcelain exterior and the inner strength of steel were particularly evidenced during the last five years of her life and her tireless work with UNICEF.

Diane Maychick in *Audrey Hepburn: An Intimate Portrait* reveals the heart and love of this woman for the starving children of the world. Ms. Hepburn's early childhood and near starvation in Holland during the Nazi invasion of World War II left an impact on her that would touch the lives of multitudes. Ms. Hepburn says of herself,

> I came from a home—a mother—who taught me first and foremost that I am secondary to other people. Service to others is what gives us meaning for ourselves. In the motion picture business, it's easy to forget your ideals. But I got out of the business, didn't do anything for much for a while, and had a lot of time to reflect on what I believed. It came down to the fact that I honored in my heart what my mother taught me. It was time to say yes to UNICEF.[19]

> I thank God now that I had this film career and that it made me so well-known. Because it's now clear to me the reason I got famous all those years ago. It was to have this career, this new one. To be able to do something—a small thing—to help people.[20]

Ms. Hepburn made over 125 field trips to such countries as Bangladesh, Vietnam, Somalia, and Ethiopia. In 1991 President George Bush presented her with the Presidential Medal of Freedom in honor of her efforts to bring relief to the needy people of the world. One friend commented about her life, "She was a healer too. If she saw someone suffering, she tried to take on their pain. She knew how to love. That's why her work with UNICEF was the perfect marriage. She couldn't stand the idea of children having pain."[21] This was a woman, bred to an aristocratic family, who enjoyed the fame and riches of world-class celebrity and yet felt her mission was to feed starving children. Like the proverbial woman, "Her hand reached out to the poor."

By the time a "woman of strength" has entered her latter years, she is characterized by both strength and dignity, a "steel magnolia." These qualities are seen in her perspective on the future, her commitment to kindness, and her constructive use of time. During this season life seems to come together for her. Her husband is now an elder (*zakem*) of the community and a significant man of public influence (Proverbs 31:23). For males, this was only possible after many years of graying and beardedness.[22] As his wife, she is also in her prime as one who will receive honor from the totality of her life.

The strength of this woman at this time is her unique future orientation. Many women do not age well. They are fearful of the future, are filled with self-hatred and regret. Olga Knopf writes,

As a matter of fact, the way in which a person reacts to internal and external changes has a greater impact on him and his personality than the changes themselves. Consequently, the way a person deals with the manifestations of his aging can make him old ahead of time or can keep him young and spry, perhaps to the very end.[23]

From the perspective of this strong woman, old age does not have to produce a negative outlook toward the future. She is not afraid of what the future may bring ("snow" in Proverbs 31:21). Her perspective on life and anticipation of the future cause her to throw back her head and laugh (verse 25). She has made peace with her past. She has accepted the pains and disappointments of the bad times along with the joys and laughter of the good times. Life this side of Heaven is paved with losing and letting go.

Writers often use the lives and accomplishments of the rich and famous to add more interest to their material. However, the lives of the ordinary people closest to us and daily little things truly impact our lives.

My mother, Ann Rosenburg, is a living example to me of the mature woman whose strength is found in her view of the future and adjustment to the past. This is a woman who still approaches life with zest and courage—who else would have taken her first ski lesson at age sixty-nine? Mom has accepted the changes in the world and made peace with the difficult, unforeseen events in her own life with strength and dignity. Her faith in God, youthful spirit, physical stamina, and wise perspective will inspire me through the rest of my life.

What is apparent in the mature woman's life is a healthy self-acceptance of her stage in life. What is sad is when women try to maintain their youthfulness beyond reason. Often the expenditure of large sums of money on plastic surgery, cosmetics, and youthful, trendy fashions only camouflages a certain self-hatred for getting old. Dr. Knopf again notes, "Sometimes the situation becomes pathetic when a person, usually a woman, does not know when to stop the attempts at rejuvenation."[24]

Self-acceptance begins when the woman can say, "I don't mind getting older, it has certain advantages like (fill in the blank)." The blanks might be filled with such comments as, "I have fewer responsibilities," "I don't have anything to prove to anybody," "I can eat what I want to eat when I want to eat it," or "It's nice to be able to send the grandchildren home at the end of the day." These realistic conceptions of the future are indeed the strengths of this woman. Rooted in complete acceptance of her age, she is in contrast to the commonly noted self-indulgent woman of the same age. Knopf comments:

> Self-acceptance is the result of a common-sense appraisal of one's faculties, advantages, and disadvantages. Self-indulgence involves self-pampering and looking for excuses to be taken care of by others instead of making use of the assets that a person still commands. Through the second course, the individual becomes a burden not only to the people in his environment but also himself, which makes the last stages of his life more painful than need be. On the other hand, self-acceptance leads to the diminution of guilt feelings and of feelings of inadequacy; it leads to lessening of tension and subsequent increase in psychic and physical energy. It also opens new avenues of self-expression that may make the last part of one's life more gratifying and more pleasant than one ever dreamed it could be.[25]

One avenue of self-expression seen in this strong woman at this late date is her desire to begin a business (Proverbs 31:24). Having learned the relational and organizational skills of running her household, she now begins to export the products of her hands to those in distant places (Canaanites). What many young women are attempting to combine in marriage, family, and work today is more easily obtained when the children are raised. This woman, apparently having raised her children, is now free to become a woman of commerce, manufacturing products which in turn can be sold and traded on the foreign markets. Her business concerns, however, do not negate her motherly concerns of still caring about her children from a distance (verse 27).[26]

Here lies another great temptation for women at this stage of the journey. The temptation to become idle once the kids are gone is apparently a very real concern in both Testaments. The text here says that she "does not eat the bread of idleness." A woman of mature strength does not waste this time in her life, sitting around the house eating and watching television all day.

In an amazing connection, the writer of this poem relates eating to idleness. How many women have become junk-food addicts simply because they have nothing else to do? One addiction counselor suggests that the essence of eating disorders lies in this passive posture of watching television. Peele writes, "TV viewing also encourages addiction because it is a passive, consumer-oriented form of entertainment. Indeed, just as excessive eating is a passive form of entertainment built around consumption, so too is the excessive drug taking and drinking."[27]

Boredom and empty, idle hours result in unproductive and wasted living. The New Testament also warns widows (who apparently don't have to work) of falling into this trap of idleness (1 Timothy 5:13). The mature woman does not eat the food driven by her passive idleness. She is still involved with life, teaching and contributing to the younger generation (Proverbs 31:26). When she opens her mouth, the wisdom she has gleaned from life's experiences flows out to those who will listen. In her relationships, she is committed to the concept of covenantal love and mercy as the rule of her life. As such, she stands in stark contrast with the odious, adulterous woman who is boisterous and brazen (7:11,13).

The writer and humorist Erma Bombeck has received publicity on her most recent book. However, the real focus of the interviews has been on her ability—despite tremendous struggles with cancer and kidney disease—to maintain and write with her characteristic humorous slant. Ms. Bombeck has kept the women of North America laughing through their years of housework and motherhood. Now, she takes women into the later years of illness and aging with that same contagious humor. She draws from an acceptance and sense of value about this season of her life. Her ability to impart wisdom through her humorous perspective serves as an encouragement and example to those who follow the same path.

In a final summary statement, this strong woman is given a universal benediction (31:28-31). As a woman of unusual strength, she is now given the praise worthy of her character and life. Her children come home to bless her (verse 28), her husband praises her (verse 28), and her accomplishments earn her the respect and tribute of the civic leaders (verse 31).[28] Even though many young daughters may have this same kind of strength, she is set above them all (verse 29). Youth is always full of energy, ambition, and strength. Where you begin is not as important as how you finish. This woman finishes well! At this stage, late in life, she is still characterized by her surpassing and surprising strength. Finishing with strength and dignity is what is important for this woman.

In the final thought, the "secret" of her strength is disclosed.

Reflecting on the young woman's beauty, the acrostic concludes, "Charm is deceitful and beauty is vain, but a woman who fears the LORD, she shall be praised" (verse 30). With this final comment, the source of her ongoing strength is revealed. She is a woman who fears the Lord, and has thus received the necessary wisdom to live life properly before both God and man (2:6-7). In all her activities, there is a God-centeredness that supplies the necessary resources for daily living.

This tribute to the strong lady of Proverbs says the senior years of a woman's life are the best. But is this true to reality? One can certainly think of the declining health, loss of functional capacities, and increased vulnerability to disease that characterize so many women. Without minimizing the people who do fall into this category, studies report a far different vision for this time of life. From Gail Sheehy's research on sixty thousand people, she concluded, "The greatest surprise of all was to find that in every group studied, whether men or women, the most satisfying stages of their lives were the later ones. Simply, older is better."[29] James Cobble concluded the same in regard to people's faith development. He writes, "My interviews indicated, that of all age groups, these individuals (mid-to-late sixties) were perhaps the most conscious of God's presence and they earnestly desired to serve Him. They truly attempted to translate faith into action."[30]

Like good wine, the soul of an aging woman can take on a more fragrant bouquet and pleasing taste. Age is not something to be feared, because it is the Lord she fears. In her reverence and submission to His plan for her, she can be the woman that He created her to be.

## A WOMAN'S UNIQUE JOURNEY

The characteristics so clearly reflected in her personhood have taken a lifetime of development. Through the seasons of life, one finds certain characteristics common to all women. These inherent qualities lie dormant and undeveloped in each young female, waiting to blossom during her journey through life.

The feminine journey finds women today traveling down a twisting, turning road that weaves into a valley and up to the mountaintop. Each woman travels her own unique road, carrying her own set of unique baggage along with the common characteristic bags of all women. Women intermingle and influence each other's journey. James Fowler believes our journey is a convergence of three influences:

"One, the direction of our personal life narrative, two, the web of social interchanges (your traveling companions) and three, one's perspectives on the divine (God's providence and grace)."[31]

Many books have been written on the stages or seasons of life, marriage, and grief. The concept of stages leads one to believe that we move from one phase to another, leaving the previous stage behind. A woman does pass through various stages or markers of development in her life's journey. Some of the characteristics that have been discussed in this book accompany her. However, the transition from stage to stage and the overlapping of stages can prove confusing and frustrating.

## THE FRUSTRATIONS OF EACH STAGE

Each stage has its own unique frustrations. The frustration for the creational woman is the difficulty in understanding equality in light of diversity, and is often experienced in trying to make one sex like the other or in feelings of inferiority due to the differences.

The young woman is frustrated by the insecurities and emotional explosions that accompany her transition. The young woman is changing from childhood to adulthood and is dealing with all the physical, emotional, and societal changes that impact her life. She is empowered by the beauty of her youth but unsure how to control it. Her self-centeredness and volatile emotions create havoc not only for herself but for those around her.

The frustrations of the nurturing woman are a result of the confusion over the significance of nurturing, particularly as a mother. The feminist movement gave women the option of exchanging the role of mother for the role of career woman. Many women want to take advantage of these opportunities for work outside of the home. Others choose to remain within the traditional role of wife and mother. Their frustration often arises from the lack of value and esteem granted to them by their female sisters as well as their male counterparts. The nurturing woman is often angry and frustrated over the divisive issue of abortion and the sanctity of life.

The frustrations of the relational woman stem from basic gender differences between men and women. The origin and reasons for these differences hinge on both biological and sociological influences. These differences are reflected in communication styles and relational needs, causing frustration and conflict within marriage and the workplace.

The frustration of the wounded woman is her powerlessness to control traumatic events that threaten her identity and her life. Women live their lives with the expectation of security, gain, and happiness. The reality is that life is primarily made up of a continual letting go, leaving, and losses. The wounds the necessary losses of life inflict cause a woman to wonder if life will ever be normal again.

The frustration of the mature woman is her confrontation with her mortality. As she approaches the end of her life, past events and relationships may take on a new perspective. Her frustrations at the aging process, the unfinished business of life, and the probability of facing the second half without a mate create new pressures and loneliness. A woman will either center the remainder of her life around herself, or she will decide to leave her mark in the lives of those around her.

## WHAT IS NEEDED AT EACH STAGE

The most difficult part of life's journey is keeping moving. It takes tremendous effort to keep moving along. At each stage there may be the temptation for a woman to just stay where she is. Lack of personal resources, voices of encouragement, and travel companions keep women stuck in the "slough of despond." Most women find they need only a friend, someone who cares, to give them the extra push down the road.

We would all agree that the road would be smoother and the pitfalls less traumatic if there were someone walking just a few feet ahead of us. Many have found this in a friend or close family member. If this is your experience, congratulations. You are a most blessed woman. With the influx of women entering the workplace and adjusting to the new responsibilities of combining work and the home, there is a strong need for the support of those who have gone before.

Joan Jeruchim and Pat Shapiro address the subject of women empowering and nurturing other women as either role models or mentors. My husband calls a mentor "a brain to pick, a shoulder to cry on, and a kick in the pants." Jeruchim and Shapiro write:

> As they progress through distinct developmental stages, women express their work identity differently in their twenties, thirties and forties. So it's clear that women need a series of role models and mentors at different ages and at different times of their development, to help them formulate their work dreams, advance in

their careers and support them as professional women. For example, if a woman is strongly focused on her career in her twenties, she may need a gung-ho-type male mentor. As she tries to combine work and motherhood in her thirties, she may prefer an older career woman with children as a mentor. Later, in her forties or fifties, she may feel ready to pass on what she knows and become a mentor to an up-and-coming woman.[32]

Such variations in mentoring are necessary for women because their development is more complex and varied than men's. While men are fathers and husbands, these roles do not interfere with their work in the same way that women's care-giving roles do. In most cases men are able to pursue their careers throughout their adult lives with few interruptions or conflicts. For women, however, every stage of adulthood contains conflicts and compromises as they balance their roles at home with those at work. Decisions such as whether to have children, when to begin a family, whether and when to work full-time, and how to find good child care must be faced and refaced. At each point, these decisions must balance with career options and family situations.[33]

The concept of mentoring, although new in the workplace, is as old as time itself. Women have always mentored each other in the basic skills of living. Even the Apostle Paul admonishes the older women of the church to mentor the younger women, particularly in the areas of marriage and parenting (Titus 2:3-6).

## EACH STAGE REQUIRES NEW EXPRESSIONS OF FAITH

The creational woman must learn to trust God with her self-image no matter how she may feel about herself. Her dignity and worth are not based on feeling worthwhile, but on the fact that she is a creation of God. She must also trust God with her deceptive, evil impulses, which can mislead her. In addition, as she grows older, she must learn to trust God with her mortality.

The young woman must learn to use her beauty to the glory of God. If she feels inferior or unattractive, she needs to trust God with His workmanship in her appearance and refuse to be caught in the trap of comparison. Those who feel they are late bloomers should be patient and wait. God has His own timetable for beauty. At a time when permissiveness prevails, they need to trust and submit to the values and standards of God, even though it may not be the popular viewpoint.

The nurturer needs to trust God with her dreams and hopes for her children. At a time when violence and tragedy pose a threat to her children and others she cares about, she needs to commit to praying for them and trusting God with them. The nurturer who works outside the home needs to be reminded of the primacy of her home and trust God with the interruptions that her family may bring to her career. For those single mothers who struggle with feelings of inadequacy and guilt, accept your limitations. Place your trust in God to fill the gap in your child's life and accept the support of others.

The relational woman needs to trust God with the many disappointments, unmet expectations, and differences that the relationship with her husband creates. She may have to trust God with her less than adequate relationships. Above all she needs to continue to trust God for her sense of identity and self-esteem. Through the dignity that is imparted to her through God's grace, she can find her well-being.

The wounded woman must call forth the toughest faith of all. In the face of failure, loss, and uncertainty, she must find comfort in a God who often does not seem to be there. Raw faith is required merely to get through the next thing. As the writer to the Hebrews says, "Faith is the assurance of things hoped for, the conviction of things not seen" (11:1).

The mature woman must trust God with her declining health, aging appearance, and diminishing abilities. If she maintains her health she may need to trust God with new opportunities for her life. At this stage it is risky to begin new things, but the mature woman trusts God and decides to "go for it"! She should be willing to be used of God and trust God for the work that He leads her to do. Her unrest, dissatisfaction, or restlessness might be traced to her "protest of the soul" in neglecting to follow the movements of the Spirit within.

Behind the scenes of a woman's journey lies the eternal God. He calls us to keep moving and desires us to keep on listening. "See to it that you do not refuse Him who is speaking" (Hebrews 12:25). As we listen, we must fix our eyes on Jesus, the author and perfecter of faith (12:2). At the end of the journey we encounter Him who has been with us every step of the way.

# NOTES

**Chapter One—A Woman's Uneasy Journey**

1. Gloria Steinem, *The Revolution from Within* (Boston, MA: Little, Brown and Co., 1991), pages 6-7.
2. Gail Sheehy, *Passages: Predictable Crises of Adult Life* (New York: Bantam, 1976), page 31.
3. Sheehy, page 31.
4. Philip Yancey, *Disappointment with God* (Grand Rapids, MI: Zondervan, 1988).
5. Nancy Groom, *From Bondage to Bonding* (Colorado Springs, CO: NavPress, 1991), page 19.
6. Quoted by Steinem, page 168.
7. M. Craig Barnes, *Yearning: Living Between How It Is and How It Ought to Be* (Downers Grove, IL: InterVarsity, 1991), page 28.
8. See James F. Cobble, *Faith and Crisis in the Stages of Life* (Peabody, MA: Hendrickson Publishers, 1985); Kenneth Stokes, ed., *Faith Development in the Adult Life Cycle* (New York: W.H. Sadlier, 1982); Urie Bronfenbrenner, *The Ecology of Human Development* (Cambridge, MA: Harvard University Press, 1979).
9. Urie Bronfenbrenner, *The Ecology of Human Development* (Cambridge, MA: Harvard University Press, 1979), page 16.
10. Sheehy, page 29.

11. Robert Hicks, *The Masculine Journey* (Colorado Springs, CO: NavPress, 1993), page 22.

## Chapter Two—Creational Woman

1. *PrimeTime Live*, July 1, 1993. Linda Ellerby was interviewed by Diane Sawyer.
2. John Naisbitt and Patricia Aburdene, *Reinventing the Corporation* (New York: Warner Books, 1985), page 242.
3. Patricia Aburdene and John Naisbitt, *Megatrends for Women* (New York: Villard Books, 1992), page xiii.
4. Aburdene and Naisbitt, *Megatrends for Women*, page xv.
5. Nancy Groom, *From Bondage to Bonding* (Colorado Springs, CO: NavPress, 1991), page 40.
6. Robert Hicks, *The Masculine Journey* (Colorado Springs, CO: NavPress, 1993), page 32.
7. *Matthew Henry's Commentary*, vol. 1 (Wilmington, DE: Sovereign Grace Publishers, 1972), page 9.
8. Larry Crabb, *Men and Women: Enjoying the Difference* (Grand Rapids, MI: Zondervan, 1991), page 142.
9. All the Old Testament patriarchs are blessed prior to their moral and spiritual failures, but no curse is ever placed on them (Noah, Genesis 9:11; Abraham, Genesis 12:2; Isaac, Genesis 26:24; Jacob, Genesis 35:9). Also, the descendants of Abraham (Israel) are blessed and thus never cursed (Genesis 12:1-6). Likewise, because in the New Testament the believer has all blessings in Christ, he or she will never be cursed (Ephesians 1:3).
10. Crabb, page 142.
11. *Theological Dictionary of the New Testament*, ed. Gerhard Friedrich, vol. 8 (Grand Rapids, MI: Eerdmans, 1972), page 40.
12. A study done by the Professional Women's Christian Fellowship in Seattle noted that women CEOs were usually characterized by their loneliness, having no significant relationships in their lives and no personal faith.
13. Hicks, page 39.

## Chapter Three—The Young Woman

1. Naomi Wolf, *The Beauty Myth* (New York: Doubleday, 1991), page 10.
2. Joe Tanenbaum, *Male and Female Realities: Understanding the Opposite Sex* (Sugarland, TX: Candle Publishing Co., 1989),

page 39.

3. Michael Strober as quoted in "How Thin Is Too Thin?" *People*, August 20, 1993, page 74.

4. "Waifs are edging out supermodels," *Philadelphia Inquirer*, May 30, 1993.

5. *Philadelphia Inquirer.*

6. *Philadelphia Inquirer.*

7. *Philadelphia Inquirer.*

8. Lois W. Banner, *American Beauty: A Social History Through Two Centuries of the American Ideal and Image of the Beautiful Woman* (New York: Alfred A. Knoff, Inc., 1983), page 9.

9. Banner, page 9.

10. *Webster's New World Dictionary* (Nashville, TN: The Southwestern Company, 1964), page 20.

11. Mary Gaitskill, "Trapped by Perfection," *Allure*, February 1993, page 66.

12. Wolf, page 6.

13. "Woman," *The New International Dictionary of New Testament Theology*, vol. 3 (Grand Rapids, MI: Zondervan, 1971), pages 1071-1073.

14. Nancy Qualls-Corbett, *The Sacred Prostitute: Eternal Aspect of the Feminine* (Toronto: Inner City Books, 1988), page 14.

15. Qualls-Corbett, pages 57-58.

16. Qualls-Corbett, pages 23-24.

17. Psychiatrist Gerald May observes, "Spiritually, addiction is a deep-seated form of idolatry. The objects of our addictions become our false gods. These are what we worship, what we attend to, where we give our time and energy instead of love. Addiction, then, displaces and supplants God's love as the source and object of our deepest true desire." (San Francisco: Harper, 1988), page 13.

18. Banner, page 3.

19. Banner, page 13; quoting *American Beauty*, page 13.

20. Banner, page 53.

21. Banner, pages 14, 16.

22. Banner, page 283.

23. Francis Brown, S.R. Driver, and Charles Briggs, *A Hebrew and English Lexicon of the Old Testament* (Oxford, England: Oxford Press, 1972), page 666.

24. William Holladay, *A Concise Hebrew and Aramaic Lexicon of the*

*Old Testament* (Grand Rapids, MI: Eerdmans, 1971), page 244.

25. The Hebrew term *zakar* has as its primary meaning "to be sharp or pointed," thus implying the clear reference to the male organ or phallus. See Brown, Driver, and Briggs, page 271.
26. Wolf, page 232. This statistic on surgery profits was found in *Standard and Poor's Industry Surveys*, 1988.
27. Wolf, page 257.
28. Robert Goldwyn, *The Patient and the Plastic Surgeon*, quoted by Kathy Healy, "Plastic Surgery Addicts," *Allure*, April 1993, page 83.
29. Some biblical scholars see in the Prophet Isaiah Satan's desire to ascend even higher than this glorious state and be like God! (See Isaiah 14:12-14.)
30. "Antiquities of the Jews," *The Works of Flavius Josephus*, tr. William Whiston (Grand Rapids, MI: Associated Publishers and Authors, Inc., n.d.), page 383.

**Chapter Four—The Nurturer**

1. Jerry J. Bigner, *Human Development: A Life-Span Approach* (New York: Macmillan, 1983), pages 142-144.
2. Carol Travis, *The Mismeasure of Woman* (New York: Simon and Schuster, 1992), pages 117-118.
3. Anne Moir and David Jessel, *Brain Sex* (New York: Bantam, Doubleday, Dell, 1989), page 147.
4. Moir and Jessel, page 131.
5. Patricia Aburdene and John Naisbitt, *Megatrends for Women* (New York: Villard Books, 1992), page 219.
6. For these differences, see Carol Gilligan, *In a Different Voice* (Cambridge, MA: Harvard University Press, 1983); Anne Moir and David Jessel, *Brain Sex* (New York: Bantam, Doubleday, Dell, 1989); Deborah Tannen, *You Just Don't Understand* (New York: Ballantine Books, 1990); Cris Evatt, *He and She* (New York: MJF Books, 1992).
7. John Naisbitt and Patricia Aburdene, *Reinventing the Corporation* (New York: Warner Books, 1985), pages 241-242.
8. Aburdene and Naisbitt, *Megatrends for Women*, page 93.
9. Charles C. Manz and Henry P. Sims, Jr., *Super-Leadership* (New York: Berkley, 1990), page xvi.
10. Moir and Jessel, page 21.
11. Joe Tanenbaum, *Male and Female Realities: Understanding the*

*Opposite Sex* (Sugarland, TX: Candle Publishing Co., 1989), pages 45-46.

12. Ben J. Wattenberg, *The Birth Dearth* (New York: Ballantine Books, 1987), page 14.
13. Wattenberg, pages 50-51.
14. Wattenberg, page 67.
15. Wattenberg, page 108.
16. *The New International Dictionary of New Testament Theology*, vol. 3, ed. Colin Brown (Grand Rapids, MI: Zondervan, 1971), page 1069.
17. Allen Ross, *Creation and Blessing* (Grand Rapids, MI: Baker Book House, 1988), page 148.
18. David Elkind, *The Hurried Child* (Reading, MA: Addison-Wesley, 1981), page 3.
19. I am not at this point making any statement about corporal punishment or spanking young children. I do believe the Scriptures have a radically different view on this subject than most of modern society. Proverbs especially condones the "controlled and purposeful" use of physical discipline (see Proverbs 23:13). However, it also puts an emphasis on being "slow to anger" (see Proverbs 15:18 and 19:11) and being a person of slow restraint (see Proverbs 17:27 and 21:23). The tragedy for children is when they are exposed to and abused by "out-of-control" mothers who are striking out as a means of releasing their inner frustrations and anxiety.
20. Jane Swigart, *The Myth of the Bad Mother* (New York: Doubleday, 1991), page 11.
21. Philip Yancy, *Disappointment With God* (Grand Rapids, MI: Zondervan, 1988), page 64.
22. In Oriental and Middle-Eastern cultures a son is under the authority of his father until he dies. Since Jesus had to be totally free of human authority, and to not discredit the customs of the day regarding sonship, Bob and I believe it was necessary that Joseph died before Jesus could begin His mission.
23. Theresa A. Rando, *Grieving* (Lexington, MA: Lexington Books, 1988), pages 164-165.

**Chapter Five—The Relational Woman**
1. Carol Gilligan, *In a Different Voice: Psychological Theory and Woman's Development* (Cambridge, MA: Harvard University Press, 1982), page 7.

2. See Susan Brownmiller, *Femininity* (New York: Fawcett Columbine, 1984), pages 207-218, for the politicization of female emotion and PMS. Although she presents much helpful historical data, the bottom line seems to say there are no real differences in the emotional lives of men and women.

3. Anne Moir and David Jessel, *Brain Sex: The Real Difference Between Men and Women* (New York: Bantam/Doubleday/Dell, 1989), pages 5, 20.

4. Moir and Jessel, page 127.

5. Moir and Jessel, page 136.

6. Moir and Jessel, page 136.

7. Moir and Jessel, page 48.

8. Moir and Jessel, page 48.

9. Gilligan, page 6.

10. Gilligan, page 42.

11. Gilligan, pages 42-43.

12. Deborah Tannen, You Just Don't Understand: Women and Men in Conversation (New York: Ballantine Books, 1990), pages 16-17.

13. Tannen, page 25.

14. Tannen, page 38.

15. Joe Tanenbaum, Male and Female Realities: *Understanding the Opposite Sex* (Sugar Land, TX: Candle Publishing, 1989), pages 114-116.

16. Richard M. Restak, *The Brain: The Last Frontier* (New York: Warner Books, 1979), page 230.

17. Quoted by Jacquelyn Wonder and Priscilla Donovan, *Whole Brain Thinking* (New York: Ballantine Books, 1984), page 12.

18. Mari Hanes, *Dreams and Delusions: The Impact of Romantic Fantasy on Women* (New York: Bantam Books, 1991), page 2.

19. Hanes, page 3.

20. Farrell, page 19.

21. Warren Farrell, *Why Men Are the Way They Are* (New York: Berkley Books, 1986), pages 18-19.

22. See Robert's book, *The Masculine Journey*, especially his material on the phallic male, for a discussion of male fantasy.

23. *The World Almanac and Book of Facts, 1992* (New York: Pharos Books, 1992), pages 311-312.

24. Eugene Monick, quoted in "Phallos and Religious Experience," *To Be a Man: In Search of the Deep Masculine*, ed. Keith Thompson (Los Angeles: Jeremy P. Tarcher, 1991), page 127.

25. Willard F. Harley, *His Needs, Her Needs* (Tarrytown, NY: Revell, 1986), page 38.
26. Harley, page 39.
27. George Gilder, *Men and Marriage* (Gretna, LA: Pelican Publishing Co., 1986), page 9.
28. Clifford and Joyce Penner, *The Gift of Sex* (Waco, TX: Word, 1981), page 209.
29. Nancy W. Denney and David Quadagno, *Human Sexuality*, second edition (Saint Louis: Mosby Year Book, 1992), page 110.
30. Clifford and Joyce Penner, *The Gift of Sex* (Waco, TX: Word, 1981), page 95.
31. Bernie Zilbergeld, *Male Sexuality* (Boston and Toronto: Little Brown, 1978), page 189.
32. Quoted in Tanenbaum, page 50.
33. Tanenbaum, pages 39, 43.
34. Tanenbaum, pages 77-79.
35. Tanenbaum, page 86.
36. See John Naisbitt and Patricia Aburdene, *Re-Inventing the Corporation* (New York: Warner Books, 1985), pages 237-265, for how women are transforming the corporate world.
37. Categories provided by Tanenbaum, pages 96-98.
38. Cris Evatt, *He and She: A Lively Guide to Understanding the Opposite Sex* (New York: MJF Books, 1992), page 149.
39. Evatt, page 154.
40. Evatt, page 42.
41. Evatt, page 44.
42. Evatt, page 48.
43. Evatt, pages 60-61.
44. Evatt, page 66.
45. Evatt, page 72.
46. Evatt, pages 74, 76.
47. Evatt, page 78.
48. Evatt, page 90.
49. Evatt, page 92.
50. Evatt, pages 104-105.
51. Evatt, page 108.
52. Evatt, page 108.
53. Evatt, pages 116-117.
54. Evatt, page 118.
55. Evatt, page 126.

56. Evatt, page 139.
57. G. J. Botterwick and Helmer Ringgren, *Theological Dictionary of the Old Testament*, vol. 1 (Grand Rapids, MI: Eerdmans, 1974), page 222.
58. Botterwick and Ringgren, page 228.
59. Colin Brown, ed., *Dictionary of New Testament Theology*, vol. 3 (Grand Rapids, MI: Zondervan, 1978), page 1062.
60. *Theological Dictionary of the New Testament*, vol. 1, word study on gune, ed. Gerhard Friedrich, (Grand Rapids, MI: Eerdmans, 1972), page 776.
61. Even though Deborah is not specifically named in this passage, she certainly gave leadership to Israel and routed armies in battle, which is commended in the text.
62. Howard and Jeanne Hendricks, ed., *Husbands and Wives* (Wheaton, IL: Victor, 1988), pages 168-170.
63. Gilligan, page 8.
64. Gilligan, page 8.
65. Nancy Groom, *From Bondage to Bonding* (Colorado Springs, CO: NavPress, 1991), page 21.
66. Groom, *From Bondage to Bonding*, page 20.
67. Henry Cloud and John Townsend, *Boundaries* (Grand Rapids, MI: Zondervan, 1992), pages 29-30.
68. Nancy Groom, *Married Without Masks* (Colorado Springs, CO: NavPress, 1989), page 21.
69. Groom, *Married Without Masks*, page 23.
70. Groom, *Married Without Masks*, page 17.

**Chapter Six—The Wounded Woman**
1. Judith Viorst, *Necessary Losses* (New York: Ballantine Books, 1987), page 3.
2. Kate Convissor, *Young Widow* (Grand Rapids, MI: Zondervan, 1992), page 47.
3. Lynn Caine, *Being a Widow* (New York: William Morrow, 1988), page 7.
4. Caine, *Being a Widow*, page 232.
5. Lynn Caine, *Widow* (New York: William Morrow, 1974), page 11.
6. Xenia Rose, *Widow's Journey* (New York: Henry Holt, 1990), page 31.
7. Rose, page 15.
8. Convissor, pages 83, 84.

9. Convissor, page 86.
10. Colin Brown, ed., *Dictionary of New Testament Theology*, vol. 3 (Grand Rapids, MI: Zondervan, 1978), page 1073. Solle writing on *chera* says the idea connotes not only the death of a husband but also the ideas of loneliness, abandonment, and helplessness.
11. Brown, page 1073; Francis Brown, S.R. Driver, and Charles Briggs, *A Hebrew and English Lexicon of the Old Testament* (Oxford, England: Oxford Press, 1972), pages 47-48.
12. Henry George Liddle and Robert Scott, *A Greek-English Lexicon* (Oxford, England: Clarendon Press, 1977), page 1990.
13. Gerhard Kittel, *A Theological Dictionary of the New Testament*, vol. 9 (Grand Rapids, MI: Eerdmans, n.d.), page 440.
14. "In fact only 11 percent of all sexual abuse is perpetrated by a stranger. The vast majority of sexually abusive events occur in relationship with a family member (29 percent) or with someone else known by the victim (60 percent)." In Dan B. Allender, *The Wounded Heart* (Colorado Springs, CO: NavPress, 1990), page 74.
15. Viktor Frankl, *Man's Search for Meaning* (New York: Washington Square Press and Pocket Books, 1984), page 64.
16. Allender, page 30.
17. Linda Sanford, *Strong at the Broken Places* (New York: Random House, 1990), page 31.
18. Allender, page 169.
19. George Barna, *The Future of the American Family* (Chicago: Moody, 1993), page 65.
20. Barna, page 68.
21. Barna, page 71.
22. Judith Wallerstein, *Second Chances* (New York: Ticknor and Fields, 1990), page xxi.
23. Wallerstein, page 42.
24. Barna, page 75.
25. Steven Nock, Sociology of the Family (Englewood Cliffs, NJ: Prentice-Hall, 1987), page 164.
26. Wallerstein, page xviii.
27. Barna, pages 81-82.
28. Robert Hicks, *Uneasy Manhood* (Nashville: Nelson, 1991), page 57.
29. Hicks, page 62.
30. Doug Sherman and William Hendricks, *Your Work Matters to God* (Colorado Springs, CO: NavPress, 1987), page 87.

31. Susan Hutchison, in a speech to the Professional Woman's Fellowship in Seattle, August 26, 1992.
32. Viorst, page 265.
33. Refer to Reddy's popular song "I Am Woman."

### Chapter Seven—Woman of Strength

1. I want to clarify two points in *Steel Magnolias* with which I disagreed. First, I found the men portrayed in the movie as weak, negative, uninvolved, and a secondary aspect of the women's lives. Unfortunately, there is often a bias in films about women against men, not portraying them in a position of positive contribution. Second, when tragedy unfolds in the movie, as in most secular films, the characters rely on the frailty of their human strength from within and from each other without acknowledging a need for divine help and presence. The viewer is left with a sense of hopelessness in dealing with the tragedies of life apart from the reality of God.
2. Ideas summarized by James F. Cobble, *Faith and Crisis: In the Stages of Life* (Peabody, MA: Hendrickson Publishers, 1985), pages 8-16.
3. John M. Rich and Joseph L. DeVitis, *Theories of Moral Development* (Springfield, IL: Charles C. Thomas, 1985), pages 88-89.
4. Carol Gilligan, *In a Different Voice: Psychological Theory and Woman's Development* (Cambridge, MA: Harvard University Press, 1982), page 74.
5. Rich and DeVitis, page 109.
6. A Hebrew acrostic takes each letter of the Hebrew alphabet and starts each verse with the sequential letter of the alphabet.
7. Francis Brown, S.R. Driver, and Charles Briggs, *A Hebrew and English Lexicon of the Old Testament* (Oxford, England: Oxford Press, 1972), pages 298-299.
8. Menachem M. Brayer, *The Jewish Woman in Rabbinic Literature: A Psychohistorical Perspective* (Hoboken, NJ: KTAV Publishing, 1986), cover page.
9. The Hebrew term *batach* is most often used of a man's trust in God, especially in the Psalms. See Harris, Archer, and Waltke, *Theological Wordbook of the Old Testament* (Chicago: Moody, 1980), pages 233-234, for more details. The word translated "gain" in the NASB is the Hebrew word *shalal*, which means spoil,

plunder, or booty, as in the spoils of war or one's private plunder. See Brown, Driver, and Briggs, pages 1021-1022.

10. The Hebrew for "considers a field," *zamam*, has the idea of considering, purposing, and devising. It denotes very purposeful action and planning. See Brown, Driver, and Briggs, page 273.

11. Please note that this tribute is still an idealized Hebrew poem and not to be understood in a narrow, literal way. I realize there are many young, frail, or incapacitated women who do not have the physical strength to do all this woman is recognized as doing. In this case, her strength is found in her fear of the Lord (Proverbs 1:20,29) and in her wisdom, both qualities of the human spirit (8:1,12-14).

12. Patricia Aburdene and John Naisbitt, *Megatrends for Women* (New York: Villard Books, 1992), page 229.

13. Gail Sheehy, *Passages: Predictable Crises of Adult Life* (New York: Bantam Books, 1977), page 500.

14. The word translated "senses" in the NASB is the Hebrew word *ta'am'*, which has the idea of taste, perceive, or examine. See Brown, Driver, and Briggs, page 381. The focus is on what one has experienced!

15. See Julias Segal, *Winning Life's Toughest Battles* (New York: McGraw-Hill, 1986), pages 53-73, for a well-documented chapter entitled "Giving Purpose to Your Pain." He notes that until people can give some purpose or meaning to their trauma, the statistics in favor of their survivablilty are not good.

16. Judith Wallerstein, *Second Chances* (New York: Ticknor and Fields, 1990), page 276.

17. The Hebrew for "stretches out her hand" picks up the Hebrew idea of spreading out widely, as in spreading out a garment or a fishing net. See Brown, Driver, and Briggs, page 831.

18. *Life Magazine: Collector's Edition*, "Life Remembers '93," "Late Greats," January 1994, page 64.

19. Diane Maychick, *Audrey Hepburn: An Intimate Portrait* (New York: Carol Publishing Group, 1993), page 228.

20. Maychick, page 228.

21. Maychick, page 225.

22. On the zaken, see Bob's book, *The Masculine Journey: Understanding the Six Stages of Manhood* (Colorado Springs, CO: NavPress, 1993), pages 149-171; and Brown, Driver, and Briggs, pages 278-279.

23. Olga Knopf, *Successful Aging: The Facts and Fallacies of Growing Old* (New York: Viking Press, 1979), page 21.
24. Knopf, page 31.
25. Knopf, page 39.
26. The Hebrew term *tzaphah*, "looks well to her household," carries the meaning of "looking after or spying out from a distance." This is the innate concern of every mother for life. She may be separated by distance but she still has her spies out, trying to see how her kids are doing! See Brown, Driver, and Briggs, page 859.
27. Stanton Peele, *The Diseasing of America: Addiction Treatment Out of Control* (Boston: Houghton Mifflin, 1989), pages 252-254.
28. The gates were often used as the place where the leaders of the nation gathered to discuss the political issues of the day. See Fred H. Wight, *Manners and Customs of Bible Lands* (Chicago: Moody, 1953), pages 239-241.
29. Sheehy, page 517.
30. Cobble, page 118.
31. James W. Fowler, *Becoming Adult, Becoming Christian* (San Francisco: Harper and Row, 1984), page 137.
32. Joan Jeruchim and Pat Shapiro, *Women, Mentors and Success* (New York: Fawcett Columbine, 1992), page 2.
33. Jeruchim and Shapiro, page 3.